Cinzia White

Twist & Turn Quilts

6 Curved-Piecing Projects

C&T PUBLISHING
Another Maker Inspired!

Text and artwork copyright © 2023 by Cinzia White

Photography copyright © 2023 by C&T Publishing, Inc.

Publisher: Amy Barrett-Daffin

Creative Director: Gailen Runge

Senior Editor: Roxane Cerda

Editor: Liz Aneloski

Technical Editor: Debbie Rodgers

Cover/Book Designer: April Mostek

Production Coordinator: Zinnia Heinzmann

Illustrator: Cinzia White, Mary E. Flynn

Photography Coordinator: Lauren Herberg

Front cover photography by Anthony Burns, Homepix Photography

Photography by Lauren Herberg, unless otherwise noted

Published by C&T Publishing, Inc., P.O. Box 1456, Lafayette, CA 94549

Library of Congress Cataloging-in-Publication Data

Names: White, Cinzia, 1958- author.
Title: Twist & turn quilts : 6 curved-piecing projects / Cinzia White.
Other titles: Twist and turn quilts
Description: Lafayette, CA : C&T Publishing, Another Maker Inspired, [2023]
  | Summary: "Challenge yourself with this intricate curved-pieced design that offers infinite possibilities and great movement in quilts. Inside features 6 quilt projects (king-size quilt, queen, double-queen quilt, two twin-size quilt, and a lap) that are all built on the same idea of interlocking paths"-- Provided by publisher.
Identifiers: LCCN 2022052613 | ISBN 9781644033111 (trade paperback) | ISBN
  9781644033128 (ebook)
Subjects: LCSH: Patchwork--Patterns. | Quilting--Patterns.
Classification: LCC TT835 .W4936 2023 | DDC 746.46/041--dc23/eng/20221114
LC record available at https://lccn.loc.gov/2022052613

Printed in China

10 9 8 7 6 5 4 3 2 1

Dedication ›››››››››››››››››››››››››››››

To my dearest husband, Paul, who has encouraged and supported me completely both in the making of these quilts and the writing of this book. Your love and support are the foundation of my world.

Acknowledgments ›››››››››››››››››››››››

To everyone involved in the making of this book, thank you. Special thanks to Liz Aneloski for your encouragement, help, and guidance throughout; Debbie Rodgers, for checking and correcting the technical aspects; April Mostek, an absolutely amazing designer; and the entire team at C&T Publishing who helped to fine-tune my ideas and bring my dream to fruition.

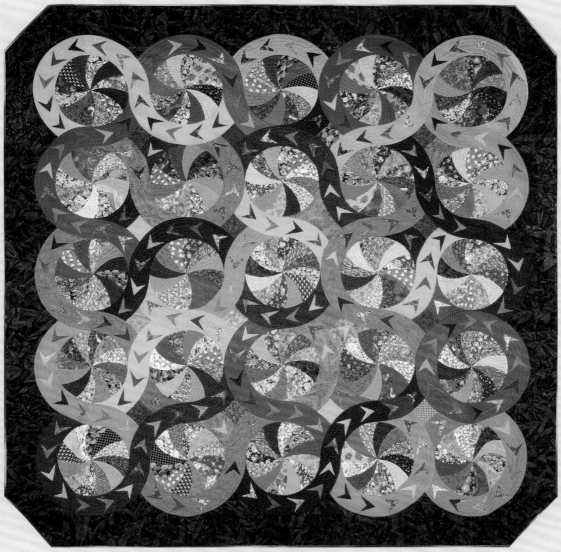

Trails

Photo by Anthony Burns, Homepix Photography

Contents

SPINNING CIRCLES 9

Photo by Anthony Burns, Homepix Photography

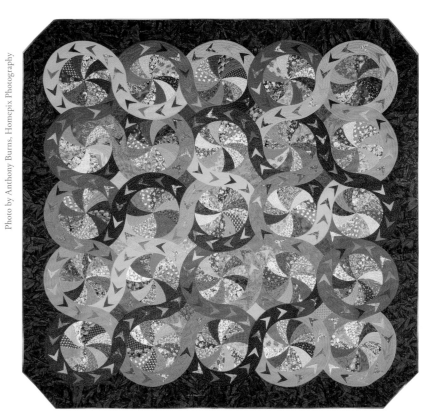

TRAILS 61

ALLEYWAY 20

LANEWAYS 25

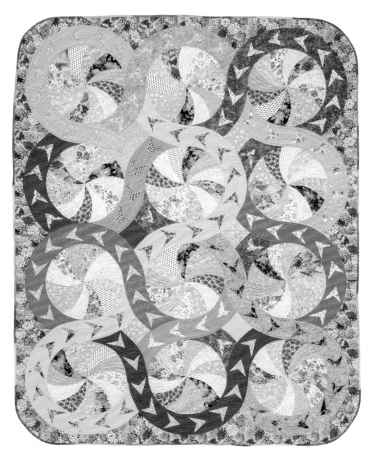

FREEWAYS 33

TRACKS 50

Introduction

Join the adventure. This design leads to a new quilt like nothing you've made before.

Too many scraps? *Trails*, *Freeways*, and *Laneways* will make a huge dent in everyone's stash.

An amazing fabric that you can't bear to cut into? *Tracks* uses huge 16″ circles as the feature.

A lover of embroidery? This too can be featured in your quilts, as in *Stroll in the Garden* (page 32).

A lover of hexagons who has never made a circular block before? Easy. Follow the detailed directions for Laneways, which utilizes a foundation paper-pieced hexagon from *The Storyteller's Sampler Quilt*, by C&T Publishing, and you can incorporate one or more of your favorite hexagonal designs.

The intertwining paths will lead the viewer's eyes to search for more. Is this one path, or is it many? How do they flow so easily?

If you want a slow, take-anywhere project, you can hand piece them. If you want it finished sooner, make these quilts using machine piecing.

Template patterns are provided for both hand and machine piecing. *Trails* was entirely hand-pieced, while the other quilts were made with a mixture of techniques, machine piecing, foundation piecing (for the circle only), and embroidery.

The detailed step-by-step instructions will guide you through every step of the process to create your own amazing quilt.

General Information

FINISHED CIRCLE: *16″ diameter* FINISHED PATH WIDTH: *4½″*

ONLINE SUPPORT

To assist with the construction of these quilts, support is offered through **facebook.com/groups/cinziawhitedesigns**

SUPPLIES AND TOOLS

Fabric

Rotary cutter, cutting mat, and quilter's ruler

Sharp scissors for cutting fabric

Template plastic

Fine permanent marker for drawing on template plastic

Scissors for cutting template plastic

Pencil for tracing templates onto fabric

Neutral-colored thread for piecing

Safety pins for securing pieces for paths and basting

Needles for hand piecing or machine sewing

Freezer paper, 18″-wide roll

Batting

Masking tape for sandwiching quilt

Sewing and quilting thread

Sandpaper board to minimize fabric movement when marking templates (optional)

Preparing the Templates

1. Trace the template patterns onto template plastic using a fine permanent marker, and transfer all markings to the template plastic.

For *hand piecing*, trace on the dashed lines (the seam allowances will be added after you trace the pattern onto the fabric).

For *machine piecing*, trace on the solid lines (the templates include the seam allowances).

2. Cut out the templates accurately along the drawn line. Label each template on the right side. Write a word beginning with the template label, rather than just the letter, so that it is easy to see when the template is reversed. Examples: Key and Lime rather than K and L.

Marking and Cutting the Fabric

For *hand piecing*, place the template faceup on the reverse side of the fabric, and trace around it using a sharp pencil. Leave ½″ between shapes cut from the same fabric to allow for the seam allowances.

For *machine piecing*, place the template faceup on the reverse side of the fabric, and trace around it using a sharp pencil. No extra fabric is needed between shapes since the seam allowances are included on the templates.

MANAGING THE PIECES

1. Cut out the pieces.

2. Lay the pieces out in order, and check for accuracy. (Does the path flow in the correct manner?) Stack the pieces from the back of the path to the front of the path, keeping all the pieces for each block together.

3. Label each path with the path number, and anchor all the pieces together with a safety pin.

4. After cutting all the main path shapes, cut the arrows (blocks A and AR) from the leftover fabrics.

Tips

GENERAL

- WOF is the width of fabric from selvage to selvage.

- LOF is the length of fabric, parallel to the selvages.

- A sandpaper board minimizes fabric movement when marking shapes.

- Cut all the fabric for each path at one time.

- You can ignore the grain lines on your fabric since the pieces are primarily curved.

- Be careful not to stretch fabric while handling and sewing.

- Select fabrics that contrast with the path and also with the nearby arrows in the same path.

HAND PIECING

- Use a thread that matches the darker of the two fabrics.

- Begin and end each line of stitching with a backstitch placed a short distance from the corner.

- Use a short running stitch.

- Always sew along the dashed lines, except for the circle center. Take extra care when approaching the center of the circle on the arcs. Sew just inside, rather than on, the marked line. Sew into the middle then back out again. Do not place a knot at the middle or double sew as this adds too much bulk.

- On long seams or bias, backstitch every 10–15 stitches to strengthen the seam and control bias stretching.

- Don't sew across seam allowances. Pass the needle through from one side to the other at the seam line.

MACHINE PIECING

- Lightly starch the fabric before cutting. Let the starch settle into the fabric for a few minutes before pressing.

- Sew using an accurate ¼″ seam allowance.

- Work with the concave curved side on top of the convex curved side.

- Gently line up the edges of the two curved pieces, right sides together, and pin the center points. Then place pins at the starting and ending points of the curve and numerous more along the entire seam.

- Use fine pins, as they don't get in the way as much as thicker pins.

- Use a shorter-than-usual stitch length—approximately 12 stitches to the inch.

- Use the needle-down setting on your machine so you always stop with the needle in the fabric.

- Sew slowly.

- Lift the foot and smooth the fabric if there is creasing while you sew the curved seam.

- Press carefully with an up-and-down motion.

Spinning Circles

FINISHED CIRCLE
16″ diameter

DESIGN AREA
72″ × 72″

FINISHED QUILT
94″ × 94″

By Cinzia White

ELEMENTS: individual curved-wedge pieced circles, background border, pieced borders, solid borders, free-motion machine quilting

This quilt provides an introduction to the curved-wedge pieced circles. Once you are familiar with this piecing, you will be ready to move onto the various paths for the remaining projects (pages 20–84).

MATERIALS

Refer to Supplies and Tools (page 7).

Fabric amounts are based on 42" width of fabric.

Black: 5⅝ yards for background, border, and binding

Florals: 42 rectangles 6" × WOF for circle wedges and sashing

¼" (6mm) iron-on quilt bias strips: 21 yards (20m)

Backing: 8⅝ yards

Batting: 100" × 100"

Posterboard/cardboard at least 16½" × 16½"

TEMPLATES

Refer to Preparing the Templates (page 7) to make Template J (page 87).

CUTTING

WOF = width of fabric

Starch and press all fabric before cutting to minimize stretching.

Black

Refer to the diagram below for cutting.

- Cut 1 rectangle 73" × WOF, subcut into 2 rectangles 73" × 21" for background. (A)

- Cut 1 rectangle 95" × WOF, subcut into 2 rectangles 95" × 6" for long borders, 4 strips 2½" × remaining WOF for binding, 1 rectangle 83" × 6" for border, 1 rectangle 73" × 21" for background, and 4 strips 2½" × remaining WOF for binding. (B)

- Cut 2 rectangles 6" × WOF for short border and 5 strips 2½" × WOF for binding. (C)

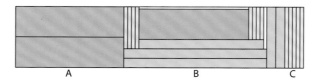

Floral fabrics

- Cut 4 pieces using template J from 42 fabrics to make 168 wedges for the circle wedges.

- Cut the remaining pieces from the 42 fabrics into 5½" rectangles.

Backing

- Cut into 3 rectangles 100" × WOF.

Making the Circles

PREPARING THE CIRCLE PATTERN

1. Draw a dashed circle with a 16" diameter on cardboard/posterboard. This is the sewing line.

2. Add a solid line ¼" outside the dashed line for the seam-allowance line around the circle. This is the cutting line.

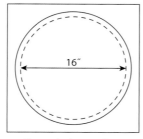

Draw circle template.

3. Check the accuracy of the drawing by tracing the dashed line of the short side of template J, 12 times, around the circle, on the dashed line for matching points.

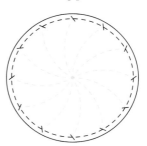

Add matching points.

SEWING THE WEDGED CIRCLES

1. Match the marked points of 2 contrasting J circle wedges.

2. Sew together.

For *hand sewing*: Sew just inside the dashed sewing lines.

For *machine sewing*: Sew using a scant ¼″ seam allowance.

3. Repeat Steps 1 and 2 to join 3 contrasting J pieces.

4. Repeat Steps 1 to 3 to make 4 of these units.

5. Sew these units together to form a circle.

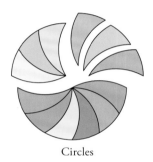

Circles

6. Make 14 circles.

7. Check to make sure they are circular, and redraw the solid cutting line if necessary. Cut on this line. They don't have to be perfect because you will be covering this raw edge with bias tape.

Layout

1. Using the quilt photo (page 9) as a guide, lay the circles on the 3 black background rectangles, and baste or glue them in place. The circles need to be secure; otherwise, they will move when you add the bias tape.

2. Working only a short distance at a time, peel back the paper backing from the bias tape, and pin or press in place to cover the edges of all the circles. Turn under any raw edges of bias tape. Where possible, hide the ends of the tape under another circle.

3. Working on 1 circle at a time, iron the bias tape in place. When completed, turn the entire piece over, and press well from the back.

4. Using a regular stitch length, sew along both edges of the tape to secure.

5. Press.

6. Repeat Steps 2–5 with all of the circles and all 3 panels.

 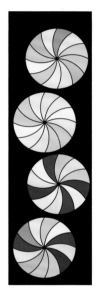 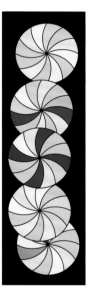

WORKING WITH FUSIBLE BIAS TAPE

- Using a craft or travel iron makes the task easier.

- Leave some extra bias at both the start and the end of the line. The ends may be trimmed after each line of bias is securely positioned.

- Center the bias on the circle edge. Check that you have completely covered all of the raw edges.

- If needed, the bias may be reheated, lifted, and repositioned before being re-ironed.

- The bias will follow the curve, but don't stretch it.

- To finish an end that isn't hidden, trim the corners of the first end, and overlap the ends approximately ½″. Fold the second end at 45°, then press and carefully trim away the excess.

Sashing and Borders

1. Measure all of the panels, and trim them if necessary so the length is the same. The panels are 21″ × 72″ but your panels may be different. Adjust borders to suit your panels.

2. Cut 5½″ floral rectangles into varying lengths between 4½″ and 18″.

3. Join the rectangles together end to end to make 4 rectangles 5½″ × 73″ (or the length measured in Step 1 + 1″) for the sashing and short borders, and 2 rectangles 5½″ × 83″ for the long sides of the center panel. All border strips are cut slightly longer than required and trimmed after being attached.

4. Matching centers, sew a pieced 5½″ × 73″ rectangle to both sides of the center panel and to the outer edge of the side panels.

5. Matching the centers lengthwise, join the 3 sections together.

6. Press the seam allowance toward the panels and trim the sashing even with the quilt panels.

7. Matching centers, sew a pieced 5½″ × 83″ rectangle to the long sides of the quilt.

8. Press the seam allowance toward the panels and trim the borders even with the quilt.

9. Join the 2 black 6″ × WOF rectangles end-to-end and trim to make a 6″ × 83″ border.

10. Matching the centers, sew each 6″ × 83″ black rectangle to the short sides of the quilt.

11. Press the seam allowance outward and trim the border even with the quilt.

12. Matching the centers, sew each 6″ × 95″ black rectangle to the long side of the quilt.

13. Press the seam allowance outward and trim.

Add borders.

>>>

Finishing the Quilt

Refer to Finishing (page 19).

QUILTING

The circles were quilted with random-sized overlapping circles, the black areas with wavy zigzags coming in from the sides, and the floral borders with free-motion flowers.

OPTIONAL: TRIMMING THE CORNERS

After completing the quilting, trim away the excess batting and backing. To trim the corners, measure 7½″ in from each corner in both directions. Draw a line directly across between these points and stitch a line of basting ⅛″ in from this line. Trim along the marked line.

BINDING THE QUILT

Using the 2½″ strips, refer to Binding (page 19).

Blocks and Terminology

The paths for *Alleyway* (page 20), *Laneways* (page 25), *Freeways* (page 33), *Tracks* (page 50), and *Trails* (page 61) are constructed using a combination of 5 blocks. The name of each block and variation refer to its location and the direction of the arrow within the path.

The Blocks

CLOCKWISE BLOCKS

Block A (arrow) uses 1 piece K and 1 piece L from the same fabric. This fabric must contrast with the surrounding path.

Block B (back) uses 1 piece S and 1 piece T from the same fabric.

Block C (core) uses 1 piece O and 1 piece P from the same fabric and 1 contrasting block A.

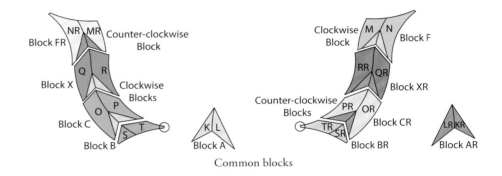

Common blocks

Block F (front) uses 1 piece M and 1 piece N from the same fabric and 1 contrasting block A.

Block X (crossover) uses 1 piece Q and 1 piece R from the same fabric and 1 contrasting block A.

COUNTERCLOCKWISE BLOCKS

Block AR (arrow reversed) uses 1 piece KR and 1 piece LR from the same fabric. This fabric must contrast with the surrounding path.

Block BR (back reversed) uses 1 piece SR and 1 piece TR from the same fabric.

Block CR (core reversed) uses 1 piece OR and 1 piece PR from the same fabric and 1 contrasting block AR.

Block FR (front reversed) uses 1 piece MR and 1 piece NR from the same fabric and 1 contrasting block AR.

Block XR (crossover reversed) uses 1 piece QR and 1 piece RR from the same fabric and 1 contrasting block AR.

-------------------------------- **Cutting** --------------------------------

- Work sequentially, following the paths, starting with the easiest construction requirements.
- Number each path as per the layout design. *Don't remove the numbers until the entire quilt top is assembled.*
- All measurements include ¼″ seam allowance.
- All fabric is cut across the width of the fabric using templates unless otherwise stated.
- I recommend that you make a circle and a sample path before cutting all of the pieces to complete the quilt.
- All templates show both the sewing line—marked with a dashed line—and the cutting line—marked with a solid line.

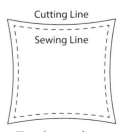

Template markings

Overview of Path Formation

On a piece of 12″ × 48″ inexpensive interfacing or paper trace around the templates to make a full-size planning sheet, showing the block relationships between each other. This is really worth the time and effort to provide an understanding of how the blocks fit together.

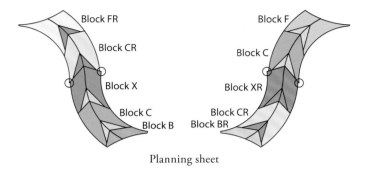

Block FR
Block CR
Block X
Block C
Block B

Block F
Block C
Block XR
Block CR
Block BR

Planning sheet

✤ Note

The center spine *must always line up, but the side does not line up between blocks X or XR and the block in front of them.* **The back and front blocks will fill this overhang when the paths are joined together. The overhang is marked with a circle in the diagrams and on the patterns.**

 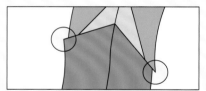

Overhang detail of crossover block

When joining a path to other paths, it is necessary to match the shortest sides first. These sides, although tiny, are important and help to align pieces.

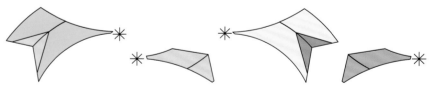

Short side of blocks are marked with *.

Block Construction

CLOCKWISE BLOCKS

1. Lay the path out entirely, with the 2 halves of each block side by side.

2. Aligning matching points, sew all pieces K and L (block A arrows) onto their adjoining path template pieces. The side marked with an arrow will always lie on the curved center spine.

Sew arrow pieces to adjoining units.

3. Starting from the back, sew the sections of each side of the path together.

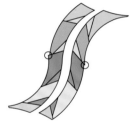

Join path sections.

4. Match the seams, and sew the 2 halves together. *If the path spine doesn't match up, check the orientation of template K/KR first. An error is easily made with this piece.*

Sew center spine.

COUNTERCLOCKWISE BLOCKS

Repeat Clockwise Blocks, Steps 1–4 (page 14), sewing pieces KR and LR (block AR-arrows) onto their adjoining path templates to complete the counterclockwise blocks.

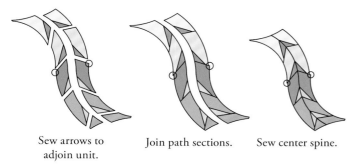

Sew arrows to adjoin unit. Join path sections. Sew center spine.

Checking the Circle Fit

Before joining all of the paths, inserts, and circles, it is a good idea to check the circle sizing.

1. Lay the prepared circle pattern (see Preparing the Circle Pattern, page 10) onto each of the completed circles, and check how they compare.

2. If the circles or segments don't line up, then draw a new circle onto the back of the completed circles using your circle template, include all of the segment marks, and use this when joining the circles to the paths.

3. *Don't trim the circles*, just sew using these lines. It is common for the circles to have slight variations.

4. Trim when the whole quilt top is finished and lying flat. My original circles were trimmed prior to joining into the quilt but were cut ½″ too small and could not be used—experience is a wonderful teacher!

5. Since the arrows don't go right to the edge of the path, it is not obvious whether the matching is seam to seam or not and it doesn't affect the final appearance.

Joining Paths and Circles

The circles are initially joined to the paths along all concave curves.

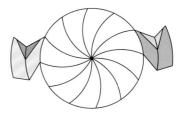

Blocks C and CR match with 1 J piece.

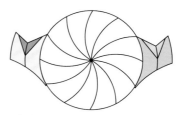

Blocks F and FR match 2 J pieces.

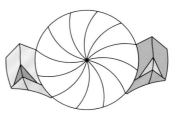

Blocks B and X, or BR and XR, match 2 J pieces.

Joining Crossover Blocks to Circles

1. Align corners and matching points on piece R (from X block).

2. Sew a J piece to the matching point of piece R.

3. Baste the remainder of the X block to the next J piece. Do not sew into the seam allowance.

4. Mark with 2 safety pins for later reference.

5. The same occurs with J pieces and piece RR.

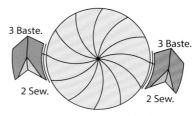

3 Baste.   3 Baste.   2 Sew.   2 Sew.

Crossover blocks and J pieces

Completing The Quilt

Background Border

PREPARING THE BACKGROUND BORDER PATTERNS

1. To obtain an accurate sewing line for the borders, first draw the full-length pattern on freezer paper.

2. Trace templates V and W (pages 91 and 92) onto template plastic using a fine permanent marker, and transfer all markings. Cut out the templates accurately along the drawn line, and label each template.

1-Circle Background Border

Use the dashed lines if hand stitching and the solid lines if machine stitching.

1. Cut a rectangle of freezer paper of the size stated in the project instructions.

2. Draw a line using a ruler of the height stated in the project instructions along one long side of the paper.

3. Fold the paper in half to locate the center.

4. Place template W on the centerline, with the short side on the fold line and the long side on the ruled line.

5. Trace template W; then reverse it, place it beside the drawn template, and trace it again; always take care to place the templates accurately.

6. Extend the sloped line to the edge of the paper. This is the joining line for the mitered corners.

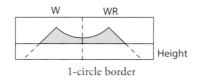
1-circle border

7. Cut along the sloped and the curved lines. Do not cut along the marked height line.

8. The pattern using the dashed lines is for the sewing lines, and the pattern using the solid lines is for the cutting lines if you're machine piecing.

2-Circle Background Border

Use the dashed lines if hand stitching and the solid lines if machine stitching.

1. Cut a rectangle of freezer paper the size stated in the project instructions.

2. Draw a line using a ruler at the stated height in the project instructions along 1 long side of the paper.

3. Fold the paper in half to locate the center.

4. Place template V on the centerline, with the tall side on the fold line and the long side of the template on the ruled line.

5. Trace template V, then reverse it, place it beside the drawn template, and trace it again.

6. Place templates W and WR on the ends of the rectangle and trace.

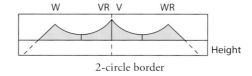
2-circle border

7. Continue as in 1-Circle Background Border, Steps 6–8 (page 16).

3-Circle Background Border

Use the dashed lines if hand stitching and the solid lines if machine stitching.

1. Cut a rectangle of freezer paper of the size stated in the project instructions.

2. Draw a line using a ruler at the stated height in the project instructions along one long side of the paper.

3. Fold the paper in half to locate the center.

4. Place template V on the centerline, with the short side on the fold line and the long side of the template on the ruled line.

5. Trace template V; then reverse it, place it beside the drawn template, and trace it again.

6. Repeat Step 5 until there are 1 full and 2 partial arcs.

7. Place templates W and WR on the ends of the rectangle and trace.

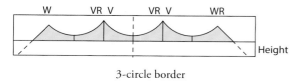

3-circle border

8. Continue as in 1-Circle Background Border, Steps 6–8 (page 16).

4-Circle Background Border

Use the dashed lines if hand stitching and the solid lines if machine stitching.

1. Cut a rectangle of freezer paper of the size stated in the project instructions.

2. Repeat as for 2-Circle Background Border, Steps 2–7 (page 16) until there are 2 full and 2 partial arcs.

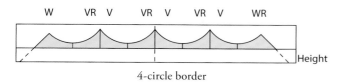

4-circle border

5-Circle Background Border

Use the dashed lines if hand stitching and the solid lines if machine stitching.

1. Cut a rectangle of freezer paper of the size stated in the project instructions.

2. Repeat as for 3-Circle Background Broder, Steps 2–8 (page 16) until there are 3 full and 2 partial arcs.

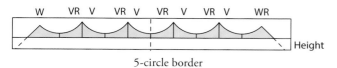

5-circle border

MARKING THE BACKGROUND BORDER

All borders are constructed in the same manner using the freezer-paper rectangles.

1. Fold the border fabric in half to find the centers, and finger-press this line.

2. Matching centers and the outer edge of the freezer-paper border, iron the freezer paper onto the wrong side of the border fabric, shiny side against the fabric. The points should be at least ¼″ from the edge of the fabric.

3. Using a fine Sakura Pigma Micron (sakuraofamerica.com) or Zig Memory System (kuretakezig.us) pen or a marking pencil, trace around the freezer paper to mark your sewing lines if you're hand piecing. If you're machine piecing, trace and cut the fabric using the solid lines.

4. Remove the freezer paper, and use it for marking the other borders, leaving at least ½″ between pieces if you're using a hand-piecing pattern. No extra fabric is needed for the machine-piecing pattern. The freezer paper may be reused several times.

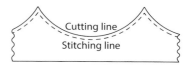

5. When ready to sew a particular arc, cut ¼″ from the marked sewing line. To minimize stretching along the bias seams, cut the curved sections only when ready to sew that particular section.

ATTACHING THE BACKGROUND BORDER

1. Lightly starch and press the fabric to minimize stretching, and pin-mark each arc of the quilt top into quarters or eighths.

Pin-mark each section.

2. Pin-mark the full arcs of the border fabric similarly.

Pin-mark full arcs of border.

3. Matching the pin marks and taking care not to stretch the fabric, sew the full arcs into place.

Sew full arcs to border.

4. Sew the miter of the borders, and pin-mark this section to match the circles. There is no matching point at the miter seam.

Join miter and pin-mark corners.

5. Sew the circles to the borders. Press the seams outward.

Sew border to quilt.

Finishing

1. Cut the selvage off, and join the backing rectangles together at the selvage using ½″ seams.

2. Press the seam to one side. Gently press the top.

3. Lay the backing right side down on a large flat surface, and tape or clip it down.

4. Layer the batting and quilt top onto the batting, gently smoothing out each layer as you go.

5. Baste the 3 layers together in a 3″ grid pattern.

QUILTING

Refer to the individual quilts for quilting suggestions.

After completing the quilting, trim the excess batting and backing even with the sides of the quilt top.

BINDING

1. Join the binding strips with diagonal seams to make one length.

2. Trim the seams to ¼″, and press open.

3. Fold the strip in half, wrong sides together, matching the long edges. Press.

4. Leaving 6″ of the end of the binding loose, stitch the binding to the edge of the quilt with a ¼″ seam, aligning the raw edges.

5. Stop ¼″ from the corner, backstitch, and fold the binding back at half the corner angle (67° for sloped corners or 45° for square corners).

Fold back.

6. With the raw edges together, fold the binding along the next side. Stitch.

Turn corner.

7. Continue to machine stitch the binding around the quilt top, matching the raw edges and mitering the corners as you go.

8. On the last side, stop sewing 12″ from the starting point.

9. Make a 45° fold at the end of the starting strip, and press.

10. Lay the folded strip end onto the other end. Mark the fold on the other end.

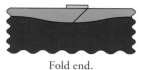

Fold end.

11. Move the binding strips away from the quilt. Match the fold line and the drawn line, and sew them together.

Join binding ends.

12. Trim the seam to ¼″. Press the seam open and refold the binding.

13. Finish sewing the binding to the quilt top.

14. Trim the batting and backing ¼″ beyond the edge of the quilt top.

15. Fold the binding to the back, and slipstitch it.

Alleyway

FINISHED CIRCLE
16" diameter

FINISHED PATH
4½" wide

DESIGN AREA
33½" × 54"

FINISHED QUILT
45½" × 66"

ELEMENTS: 2-circle curved-wedge pieced layout, clockwise and counterclockwise paths, background border, solid borders, free-motion machine quilting

By Cinzia White

Terminology

To understand the abbreviations and construction it is important that you read Preparing the Templates (page 7), The Blocks (page 13), and Overview of Path Formation (page 14).

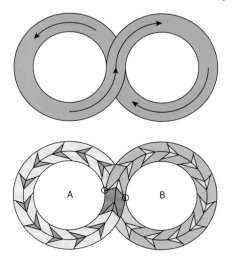

TEMPLATES

Make templates for:

- J for the circle wedges
- K and L for blocks A and AR
- S and T for blocks BR
- O and P for blocks C and CR
- M and N for block F
- Q and R for block XR

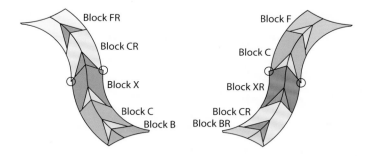

MATERIALS

Refer to Supplies and Tools (page 7).

Fabric amounts are based on 40″ width of fabric.

Purple tone-on-tone: 1¼ yards for path and binding

Green tone-on-tone: 12 fabrics; 2 squares 9″ × 9″ of each fabric for circle wedges, block AR, and block A

Green batik: 2⅛ yards for background border and outer border

Green floral: ⅝ yard for Border 2

Backing: 3 yards

Batting: 51″ × 71″

SUPPLIES AND TOOLS

See General Information; Supplies and Tools (page 7).

Freezer paper, 18″-wide: 2⅝ yards

CUTTING

WOF = width of fabric.

Starch and press all fabric before cutting to minimize stretching.

Always mark the center spine with an arrow; it is marked with a double-ended arrow on the template. Refer to The Blocks (page 13) for more information.

Purple tone-on-tone

- Cut 1 block BR, 10 block CR, 1 block XR, 10 block C, and 1 block F for the path.
- Cut 6 strips 2½″ × WOF for binding.

Green tone-on-tone

- From *each* set of squares cut 2 circle wedge J, 1 piece using template L, 1 piece using template K for 1 A block, and 1 piece using template LR and 1 piece using template KR for 1 AR block to yield 24 circle wedges and 12 each of pieces L, LR, K, and KR.

Green batik

- Cut 5 rectangles 3½″ × WOF.

  Set aside the remainder for the background border.

Green floral

- Cut 5 rectangles 3½″ × WOF.

Circles

Referring to Making the Circles (page 10), make 2 pieced circles.

>>

Path

Refer to Block Construction (page 14).

1. Lay out the fabric pieces for 1 block BR, 10 block CR, and 1 block XR in order. There will be 1 extra of L, LR, K, and KR.

2. Sew the arrows to the neighboring unit.

Sew arrows to units.

3. Working from the back, join units of one side first, then the other. Note the center spine must always line up, but the outer edges between block X and block CR do not line up.

Join units.

4. Sew the 2 halves together joining the BR block short side to the XR block overhang only. *If the path spine doesn't match up, check the orientation of template K/KR first. An error is easily made with this piece.*

Counterclockwise path

5. Lay out the fabric pieces for 10 block C and 1 block F in order.

6. Sew the arrows to the neighboring unit.

7. Working from the back, join units of one side first, then the other.

Join units.

8. Sew the 2 halves together, joining the F block short side to the C block overhang only.

Clockwise path

Joining Path and Circles

Refer to Joining Paths and Circles (page 15) and Joining Crossover Blocks to Circles (page 15).

1. Match the seams between circle A; 10 J pieces; the counterclockwise path; and the CR blocks. Sew.

2. Match the short side of the BR block to the XR block front.

3. Match circle A, 2 J pieces, to the midpoint of XR and BR blocks. Sew.

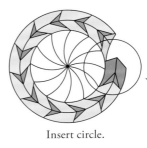

Insert circle.

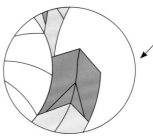

4. Match the seams between circle B, 12 J pieces, and the clockwise path, CR and F blocks. Sew.

5. Match the center spine of both sections.

6. Match the BR block short side, and the C block back, to the XR block front, and the F block short side. Sew.

7. Sew the BR block back to the clockwise circle outer curve.

8. Sew the F block to the counterclockwise circle, outer curve.

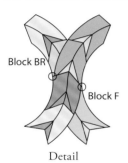

Detail

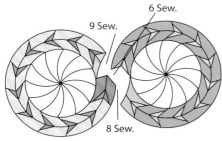

Join paths together.

9. Lay this center section on a flat surface. If it's not flat, then adjust before continuing. Adjust the seam widths between the circles as needed.

Borders

BACKGROUND BORDER

Refer to Preparing the Background Border Patterns (page 16).

1. Cut a rectangle of freezer paper 10″ × 36″.

2. Draw a line with a ruler 2″ from a long edge.

3. Draw a 1-circle border (page 16).

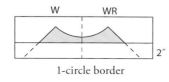

1-circle border

4. Cut a rectangle of freezer paper 10″ × 56″.

5. Draw a line with a ruler 2″ from a long edge.

6. Draw a 2-circle border (page 16).

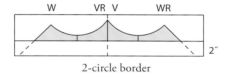

2-circle border

Cutting

Refer to Marking the Background Border (page 17).

Starch and press all fabric before cutting to minimize stretching.

1. Press the 2-circle background border freezer-paper template to the wrong side of the fabric rectangle. Trace around the template. The dashed line is the sewing line. The solid line is the cutting line.

2. Leaving at least ½″ between the sewing lines, trace around the 2 background border freezer-paper templates again.

3. Repeat Steps 1 and 2 with the 1-circle border freezer-paper template twice.

4. Cut ¼″ from the sewing line of the borders when ready to sew.

Adding the Background Border

Refer to Attaching the Background Border (page 18). The quilt top measures 25½″ × 46″ before adding the background borders.

Note

The mitered corners of the background border are joined prior to sewing it onto the quilt center. Join the path sections.

1. Sew all mitered seams together.

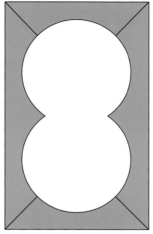

Sew mitered corners.

2. Working around each circle separately, pin-mark into eighths. There is no pin mark at the miter seam.

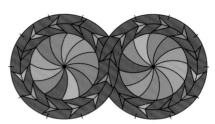

Pin-mark into eighths.

3. Pin-mark each path's outer edge in eighths.

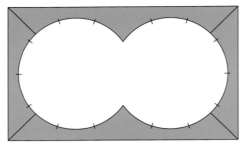

Pin-mark border.

4. Match the pins. Sew. Press seams outward. The quilt top measures 33½″ × 54″.

Sew border to quilt.

BORDER 2

1. Join all 3½″ Border 2 rectangles together end-to-end into one long rectangle.

2. Measure the quilt top through the center lengthwise. It was 54″ for this quilt.

3. Add 1″ to the measurement, and cut 2 border rectangles to this measurement.

4. Place a pin ½″ from each end, in the center of the rectangle, and halfway between each of the other pins. The rectangle is pinned at quarter points, ignoring the ½″ at both ends.

5. Pin-mark the sides of the quilt top in quarters.

6. Pin the borders to the quilt top, matching the pin marks, and stitch into place.

7. Press the seams outward.

8. Trim the border even with the quilt top.

9. Measure the quilt top through the center, side to side. It was 39″ in this quilt.

10. Add 1″ to the measurement, and cut 2 border rectangles to this measurement.

11. Repeat Steps 4–8 to attach these borders.

12. Press and square up the quilt. This quilt measured 39½″ × 60″ at this stage.

OUTER BORDER

1. Using the 3½″ green batik rectangles, repeat Steps 1–12 of Border 2.

2. This quilt measured 45½″ × 66″ at this stage.

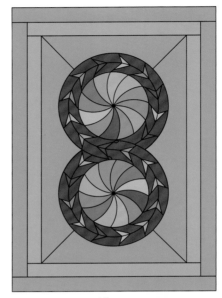

Alleyway

Finishing the Quilt

1. Cut the backing fabric into 2 pieces.

2. Refer to Finishing (page 19).

QUILTING

The circles were quilted using random-sized overlapping circles; the lanes were quilted with wavy lines accentuating the arrow direction; the first batik and floral borders were quilted with free-motion flowers, treating the 2 borders as one area and the outer batik was quilted with the same wavy lines as the paths but this time they resemble spikes coming from the outer edge.

BINDING THE QUILT

Refer to Binding (page 19).

Laneways

FINISHED CIRCLE
16″ diameter

DESIGN AREA
38½″ × 79½″

FINISHED LANEWAY
4½″ wide

FINISHED QUILT
70″ × 93″

By Cinzia White

ELEMENTS: 3-circle foundation-pieced-wedge layout, multicolored clockwise and counterclockwise paths, scrappy foundation-pieced background border, pieced borders, free-motion machine quilting.

Terminology

To understand the abbreviations and construction, it is important that you read Preparing the Templates (page 7), The Blocks (page 13), and Overview of Path Formation (page 14).

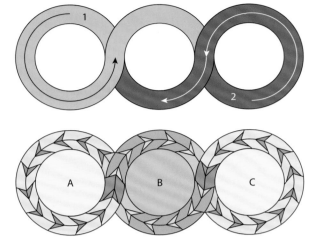

Templates

Make templates for:

- K and L for blocks A and AR
- S and T for block BR
- O and P for blocks C and CR
- M and N for block F
- Q and R for block XR

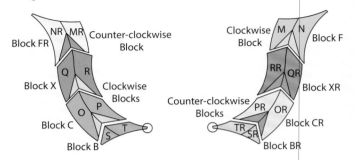

MATERIALS

Refer to Supplies and Tools (page 7).

Fabric amounts are based on 40″ width of fabric.

Scraps: approximately 3 yards for the spiral circles, arrows, and background border or 2½ yards of stripe fabric

Gray tone-on-tone scraps: 2¼ yards total for paths and border 2

Purple tone-on-tone: 7 rectangles 6″ × WOF and 4 rectangles 7″ × WOF or 2 yards for Borders 2 and 3

Green batik: ⅔ yard for Border 4

Blue batik: ⅓ yard for Border 4

Backing: 5⅔ yards

Batting: 76″ × 99″

Red tone-on-tone: ¾ yard for binding

SUPPLIES AND TOOLS

See General Information; Supplies and Tools (page 7).

Freezer paper, 18″-wide: 3⅓ yards

CUTTING

WOF = width of fabric.

Starch and press all fabric before cutting to minimize stretching.

Always mark the center spine with an arrow; it is marked with a double-ended arrow on the template. Refer to The Blocks (page 13) for more information.

Scrap fabric

Each arrow is made of 2 pieces of the same fabric.

- Cut 10 A blocks and 22 AR blocks from a variety of scraps.
- Cut strip sizes as noted on the patterns for the circles.
- Cut strips in varying widths × 14″ in length for the background border.

Scraps

- Cut a large variety of scraps in varying widths and lengths for the background border. The widths are between 1½″ and 3″. The length of the strip must be at least 1″ longer than where it will be used on the border. Read all of the instructions for the border before cutting. Starch and press all fabric before cutting to minimize stretching. When sewn side by side, these strips need to be approximately 6 yards long.

Gray tone-on-tone

All blocks have 2 different gray pieces and one colored arrow.

From each gray fabric cut 2 or 3 blocks.

- Cut 12 rectangles 6″ × WOF for spirals, paths, and Border 2.

  Subcut 1 block BR, 10 block CR, 1 block XR, 4 block C, and 1 block F for Laneway 1.

  Subcut 1 block BR, 10 block CR, 1 block XR, 4 block C, and 1 block F for Laneway 2.

  From the remaining fabric, cut 1 strip 1¾″ × width of remaining length for spirals. Cut more as needed.

  Subcut strips 2½″ × remaining lengths for Border 2 (approximately 9 yards in length).

Purple tone-on-tone

- Cut 7 strips 2½″ × WOF for Border 2 and short Border 3.
- Cut 15 rectangles 3½″ × WOF for Border 3 (total length is approximately 15 yards).

Green batik

- Cut 6 rectangles 3¼″ × WOF for Border 4.

Blue batik

- Cut 3 rectangles 3¼″ × WOF for Border 4.

Red tone-on-tone

- Cut 9 strips 2½″ × WOF for binding.

Spiral Circles

1. Copy Laneways patterns A and B onto lightweight paper (pages 93 and 94). Make 9 copies of each.

2. Fabric strip sizes are written on the pattern. Cut scrap strips, and lay them on the paper to check the arrangement. S denotes spiral circle fabric, and B denotes background fabric.

3. Foundation piece the triangles using your preferred method.

4. Press and trim the outer triangle. *Don't* trim along curved lines. These are only to show the approximate finished size.

5. Join the triangles to form a hexagon. Make 3 hexagons.

Make 3.

6. Refer to Making the Circles (page 10) to make the circle template. On the reverse of the fabric, draw a circle; include all markings. Don't trim at this stage.

Laneways

Refer to Block Construction (page 14).

1. Lay out the fabric pieces for 1 block BR, 10 block CR, 1 block XR, 4 block C, and 1 block F in order. Use 2 different gray tone-on-tone fabrics for each block.

2. Sew the arrows to the neighboring unit.

Sew arrows to units.

3. Working from the back, join the units of one side first, then the other. Note that the center spine must always line up, but the outer edges between block X and CR do not line up.

Join the units.

4. Sew the 2 halves together to complete Laneway 1. *If the path spine doesn't match up, check the orientation of Template K/KR first. An error is easily made with this piece.*

Laneway 1

5. Match the XR block overhang to the BR block short side.

6. Sew the back of Laneway 1 to the outer curve of Laneway 1 to complete the circle.

7. Repeat Steps 1–6 for Laneway 2.

JOINING LANEWAYS AND CIRCLES

Refer to Joining Paths and Circles (page 15), Joining Crossover Blocks to Circles (page 15), and the quilt photo (page 25).

1. Pin-mark each circle section into quarters. Pin-mark the midpoint of each C and CR block.

2. Note that an XR block sewn to a BR block is the same as 2 CR blocks. Pin-mark the quarter points of the XR–BR combinations.

3. Place circle A so the midpoint of the Laneway 1, CR blocks, matches with the midpoint of the circle sections. The circle quarter points match with the seams between the path sections. Match all pins, and sew.

Detail

Insert circle.

4. Repeat Step 3 with circle C and Laneway 2.

5. Match Laneway 1, C block overhang, to Laneway 2, F block, short side.

6. Sew Laneway 2 front to Laneway 1 outer curve.

7. Match Laneway 2, C block overhang, to Laneway 1, F block, short side.

8. Sew Laneway 1 front to Laneway 2 outer curve.

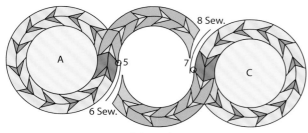

Join paths.

9. Repeat Step 3 to sew circle B to the lanes.

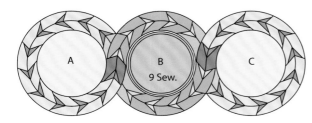

Insert circle.

10. Lay your quilt top on a flat surface. If it does not lie flat, check to see where seams have not been sewn correctly, and restitch.

Borders

BACKGROUND BORDER

Patterns

Refer to Preparing the Background Border Patterns (page 16).

1. Cut a rectangle of freezer paper 10″ × 40″

2. Draw a line with a ruler 4½″ from a long edge.

3. Draw a 1-circle border following directions (page 16).

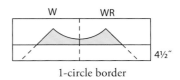

1-circle border

4. Cut a rectangle of freezer paper 10″ × 80″.

5. Draw a line with a ruler 4½″ from a long edge.

6. Draw a 3-circle border following directions (page 16).

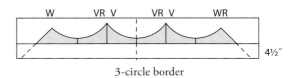

3-circle border

Piecing the Background Border

Starch and press all fabric before cutting to minimize stretching.

The border was sewn using the freezer-paper foundation piecing method in which the paper is NOT sewn through. It is not necessary to draw any stitching lines for the rectangles. The paper provides a guide to the size of the shape needed. If you prefer, you can piece through regular foundation paper.

1. Lay a strip of fabric 1, right side down on the ironing board. Place the end of the prepared freezer-paper border pattern shiny side down on the strip, with the fabric extending at least ½″ on all sides. Using a warm DRY iron, press the freezer paper to the fabric.

Press fabric to freezer paper.

2. Pull the fabric free from the freezer paper ½″ along the side to be sewn to expose the seam allowance. Fold the freezer paper back to form a crease.

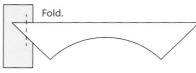

Crease freezer paper.

3. Lay a strip of fabric 2, right side up on the table, and align the sewing edge with fabric 1 edge. Pin.

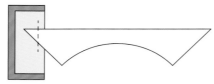

Align fabric edges.

4. Fold the freezer paper back along the formed crease. Using a slightly shorter-than-usual stitch length, approximately 12 stitches to the inch, and starting at the edge of the fabric before the freezer-paper edge, stitch right beside the freezer-paper crease. Don't stitch through the paper.

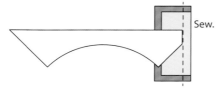

Stitch beside freezer paper.

5. Fold fabric 2 over, and using a warm, dry iron, press the fabric onto the freezer paper.

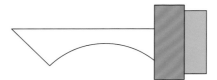

Press fabric to freezer paper.

6. Repeat Steps 2–5 until the entire border strip is covered.

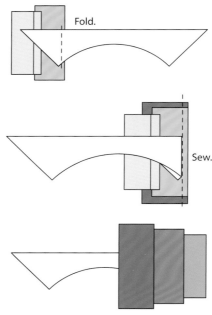

Repeat with other fabrics.

7. Lightly spray starch the fabric, right side up, and press.

8. Turn it over to the wrong side and stitch along the stitching line, just beside the paper, to minimize stretching. The dashed line is the sewing line. The solid line is the cutting line.

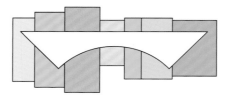

Stitch around template.

9. Repeat for all of the borders.

10. Trim ¼″ from the sewing line of the borders when you are ready to sew.

Adding the Background Border

Refer to Attaching the Background Border (page 18). The quilt top measures 38½" × 79½".

BORDER 2

1. Join the 2½" gray strips end to end, using 45° seams. Press and cut the 4 strips 80½" long.

2. Sew the 2 strips together lengthwise. Press. Make 2 sets.

3. Mark the complete quilt length on the strip starting ½" from one end. Pin-mark both border and quilt into quarters, match, and stitch together. Press seam allowance outward, and trim borders. Top measures 46½" × 79½".

4. Join 3 purple 2½" strips end to end, using 45° seams. Press and cut the 2 strips 48" long.

5. Repeat Step 3, and sew the strips to the short sides of the quilt.

BORDER 3

1. Join the 3½" purple rectangles end to end, using 45° seams. Press and cut the 6 rectangles 85" long.

2. Sew 3 rectangles together lengthwise. Press. Make 2 sets.

3. Measure the quilt length, and mark this length on the rectangle starting ½" from the end. Pin-mark both the border and quilt into quarters, match, and stitch together. Press the seam allowance outward.

4. Join 4 purple 2½" strips end to end, using 45° seams. Press and cut the 2 strips 66" long.

5. Repeat Step 3, and sew the strips to the short sides of the quilt.

BORDER 4

1. Sew the blue 3¼" rectangles end to end. Press and cut 1 rectangle 60" and 1 rectangle 50".

2. Sew the green 3¼"rectangles end to end. Press and cut 1 rectangle each of 89", 71", 40", and 30".

3. Sew the 60" blue rectangle and 40" green rectangle end to end using a 45° seam. Repeat with the 50" blue and 30" green rectangles.

4. Adjusting the placement of the 2 colored borders as shown in the photo, sew the long rectangles to the sides of the quilt. Press the seam allowances outward, and trim even with the quilt.

5. Repeat with the short borders. The quilt measures 70" × 93".

Finishing the Quilt

1. Cut the backing fabric into 2 pieces.

2. Refer to Finishing (page 19).

QUILTING

The main section lines, spiral circles, lanes and arrows were ditch stitched as well as approximately every 8" along the border. Wavy lines echo the path direction in the gray paths section. A series of echoed triangles fill the striped border, an echoed braid is in the gray borders, free-motion flowers fill the purple borders, and a wavy zigzag line is in the outer border.

BINDING THE QUILT

Refer to Binding (page 19).

Stroll in the Garden

Stroll In the Garden, 34½″ × 71″, by Verlie Gabrio 2021

MATERIALS

Refer to Supplies and Tools (page 7).

Fabric amounts are based on 40″ width of fabric.

Maroon tone-on-tone: 1 yard for laneways

White tone-on-tone: 1 yard for circles

Floral: 3 yards for border, arrows, and binding

Backing: 2¼ yards

Batting: 41″ × 77″

SUPPLIES AND TOOLS

See General Information; Supplies and Tools (page 7).

Freezer paper, 18″-wide: 3⅓ yards

CONSTRUCTION

Stroll in the Garden is made following the steps of *Laneways* (page 25), using a variety of embroidery patterns for the circles and a plain border.

BORDER PATTERNS

Refer to Laneways, Background Border (page 29) however in Patterns, Step 2 (page 29), draw a line with a ruler 2½″ from a long edge.

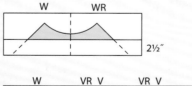

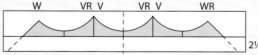

Freeways

FINISHED CIRCLE
16″ diameter

DESIGN AREA
66½″ × 87″

FINISHED FREEWAYS
4½″ wide

FINISHED QUILT
71½″ × 92″

ELEMENTS: 12 curved-wedge pieced circles, one-color clockwise and counter-clockwise paths, background border, free-motion machine quilting

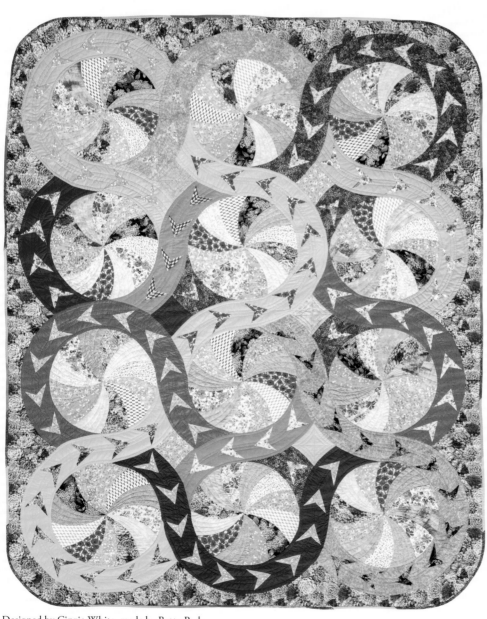

Designed by Cinzia White, made by Betty Park

Terminology

To understand the abbreviations and construction, it is important that you read Preparing the Templates (page 7), The Blocks (page 13), and Overview of Path Formation (page 14).

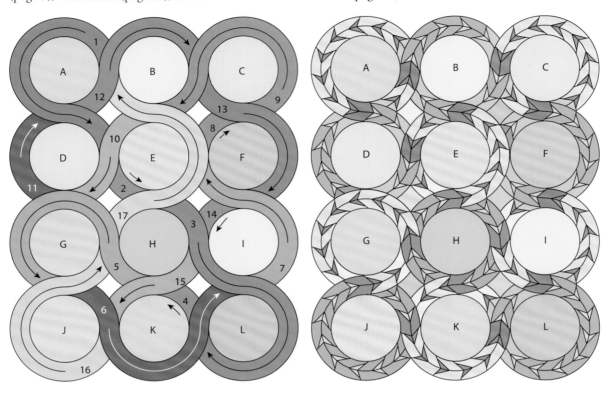

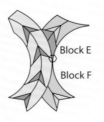

✿Note

The paths are constructed using a combination of 5 basic blocks and one variation, block E (extended back). Information about the basic blocks is provided in The Blocks (page 13).

Freeways 7 and 8 in *Freeways* do not cross another path. This creates a variation for the back block in Freeway 8, requiring a slight extension to the short side. This block is block E (extended back) and uses one piece using Template S and one piece using Template U from the same fabric.

The point where the front (block F) and the extended back (block E) meet is marked with a hexagon.

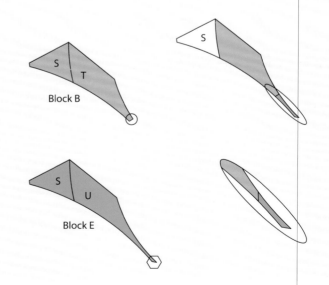

Templates

Make templates for:

- K and L for blocks A and AR
- S and T for blocks B and BR
- O and P for blocks C and CR
- S and U for block E
- M and N for blocks F and FR
- I for the insert
- J for the circle wedges
- Q and R for blocks X and XR

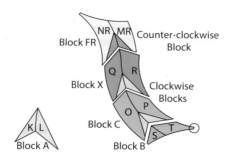

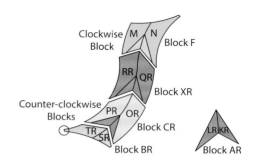

MATERIALS

Refer to Supplies and Tools (page 7).

Fabric amounts are based on 40″ width of fabric.

Blue: ⅞ yard for Freeways 1 and 13

Purple tone-on-tone: ⅞ yard for Freeways 2, 4, 8, 9, and 14

Green tone-on-tone: 1 yard for Freeways 3 and 12

Dark pink: ⅞ yard for Freeways 5 and 7

Dark purple: ⅔ yard for Freeways 6 and 11

Orange: ½ yard for Freeways 10 and 15

Yellow: 1 yard for Freeways 16 and 17

Arrow fabrics:

- 2″ × 8″ each for Freeways 2, 4, 8, 14
- 4″ × 15″ each for Freeways 10, 11, 15
- 7″ × 15″ each for Freeways 7, 12, 13
- 8″ × 22″ each for Freeways 1, 3, 5, 6, 9, 16, 17

20 assorted fabrics: ¼ yard each for the curved circle wedges and inserts

Background border: 2¾ yards

Backing: 5½ yards

Binding: Scraps from the quilt: 28 strips 2½″ × 12″ for binding along straight edges

Purple: 1 fat quarter for bias binding on the curved corners

Batting: 78″ × 98″

SUPPLIES AND TOOLS

See General Information; Supplies and Tools (page 7).

Freezer paper, 18″-wide: 2¾ yards

CUTTING

Starch and press all fabric before cutting to minimize stretching.

Always mark the center spine with an arrow; it is marked with a double-ended arrow on the template. Refer to The Blocks (page 13) for more information.

Blue

- Cut 1 block BR, 7 block CR, 1 block XR, 1 block C, and 1 block F for Freeway 1.
- Cut 1 block BR, 1 block CR, 1 block XR, 4 block C, and 1 block F for Freeway 13.

Purple tone-on-tone

- Cut 1 block BR and 1 block FR for Freeway 2.
- Cut 1 block BR and 1 block FR for Freeway 4.
- Cut 1 block E and 1 block F for Freeway 8.
- Cut 1 block BR, 7 block CR, 1 block XR, 1 block C, and 1 block F for Freeway 9.
- Cut 1 block BR and 1 block FR for Freeway 14.

Green tone-on-tone

- Cut 1 block B, 1 block C, 1 block X, 2 block CR, 1 block XR, 7 block C, and 1 block F for Freeway 3.
- Cut 1 block BR, 1 block CR, 1 block XR, 4 block C, and 1 block F for Freeway 12.

Dark Pink

- Cut 1 block B, 1 block C, 1 block X, 7 block CR, and 1 block FR for Freeway 5.
- Cut 1 block BR, 4 block CR, 1 block XR, 1 block C, and 1 block F for Freeway 7.

Dark Purple

- Cut 1 block B, 1 block C, 1 block X, 5 block CR, 1 block XR, 1 block C, and 1 block F for Freeway 6.
- Cut 1 block E, 3 block C, and 1 block F for Freeway 11.

Orange

- Cut 1 block BR, 1 block CR, 1 block XR, 1 block C, and 1 block F for Freeway 10.
- Cut 1 block B, 1 block C, 1 block X, 1 block CR, and 1 block FR for Freeway 15.

Yellow

- Cut 1 block B, 7 block C, 1 block X, 1 block CR, and 1 block FR for Freeway 16.
- Cut 1 block B, 1 block C, 1 block X, 5 block CR, 1 block XR, 1 block C, and 1 block F for Freeway 17.

Assorted fabrics

- Cut 144 pieces using Template J for the circle wedges.
- Cut 6 pieces using Template I for the inserts.

Circles

Referring to Making the Circles (page 10), make 12 pieced circles.

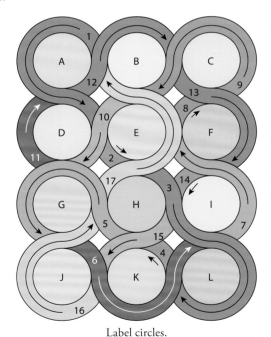

Label circles.

Freeways

FREEWAY 2

1. Lay out the fabric pieces for 1 block BR and 1 block FR in order.

2. Referring to Block Construction (page 14), complete Freeway 2.

3. Make 3 for Freeways 2, 4, and 14.

Freeways 2, 4, and 14

FREEWAY 8

1. Lay out the fabric pieces for 1 block E and 1 block F in order.

2. Referring to Block Construction, Counterclockwise Blocks (page 15) complete Freeway 8.

Freeway 8

FREEWAY 11

1. Lay out the fabric pieces for 1 block E, 3 block C, and 1 block F in order.

2. Referring to Block Construction, Counterclockwise Blocks (page 15), complete Freeway 11.

Freeway 11

FREEWAY 10

1. Referring to Block Construction (page 14), complete Freeway 10.

2. Lay out the fabric pieces for 1 block BR, 1 block CR, 1 block XR, 1 block C, and 1 block F in order.

---

3. Sew arrows to a neighboring unit.

4. Working from the back, join units of one side first, then the other. Note the center spine must always line up, but the outer edges between block X and block CR do not line up.

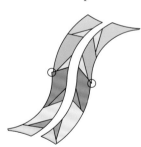

5. Sew the 2 halves together to complete Freeway 10. *If the Freeway spine doesn't match up, check the orientation of Template K/KR first. An error is easily made with this piece.*

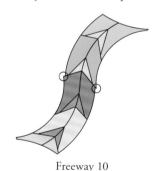

Freeway 10

FREEWAY 15

1. Lay out the fabric pieces for 1 block B, 1 block C, 1 block X, 1 block CR and 1 block FR in order.

2. Referring to Block Construction, Counterclockwise Blocks (page 15), complete Freeway 15.

Freeway 15

FREEWAY 1

1. Lay out the fabric pieces for 1 block BR, 7 block CR, 1 block XR, 1 block C, and 1 block F in order.

2. Referring to Block Construction (page 14), complete Freeway 1.

3. Make 2 for Freeways 1 and 9.

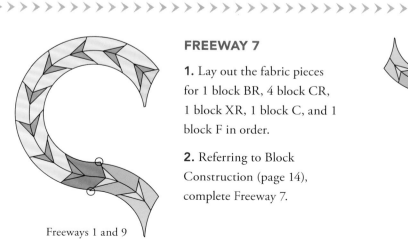

Freeways 1 and 9

FREEWAY 7

1. Lay out the fabric pieces for 1 block BR, 4 block CR, 1 block XR, 1 block C, and 1 block F in order.

2. Referring to Block Construction (page 14), complete Freeway 7.

Freeway 7

FREEWAY 12

1. Lay out the fabric pieces for 1 block BR, 1 block CR, 1 block XR, 4 block C, and 1 block F in order.

2. Referring to Block Construction (page 14), complete Freeway 12.

3. Make 2 for Freeways 12 and 13.

Freeways 12 and 13

FREEWAY 5

1. Lay out the fabric pieces for 1 block B, 1 block C, 1 block X, 7 block CR, and 1 block FR in order.

2. Referring to Block Construction, Counterclockwise Blocks (page 15), complete Freeway 5.

Freeway 5

FREEWAY 16

1. Lay out the fabric pieces for 1 block B, 7 block C, 1 block X, 1 block CR, and 1 block FR in order.

2. Referring to Block Construction, Counterclockwise Blocks (page 15), complete Freeway 16.

Freeway 16

FREEWAY 6

1. Lay out the fabric pieces for 1 block B, 1 block C, 1 block X, 5 block CR, 1 block XR, 1 block C, and 1 block F in order.

2. Referring to Block Construction, Counterclockwise Blocks (page 15), complete Freeway 6.

3. Make 2 for Freeways 6 and 17.

Freeways 6 and 17

FREEWAY 3

1. Lay out the fabric pieces for 1 block B, 1 block C, 1 block X, 2 block CR, 1 block XR, 7 block C, and 1 block F in order.

2. Referring to Block Construction, Counterclockwise Blocks (page 15), complete Freeway 3.

Freeway 3

Joining Freeways, Inserts, and Circles

Refer to Joining Paths and Circles (page 15) and Joining Crossover Blocks to Circle (page 15).

Some seams are initially basted as there is only one definite matching point. Place 2 safety pins in these seams to make it easy to find them again later.

Later, when joining to places that have only been basted, sew the original seams securely.

Sew an insert to Freeways 2, 4, 8, and 14.

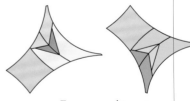

Freeway and insert

UNIT FA

1. Match circle A, 8 J pieces, to Freeway 1, 7 CR blocks and up to the matching point of the XR block.

2. Baste circle A to Freeway 1, BR block.

3. Sew circle A, 8 J pieces, to Freeway 1, 7 CR blocks and up to the matching point of the XR block.

4. Baste circle A to Freeway 1, remainder of the XR block.

5. Label this Unit FA.

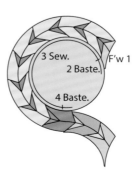

Unit FA

UNIT FB

1. Sew circle B, 6 J pieces, to Freeway 12, 4 C, and 1 F block.

2. Label this Unit FB.

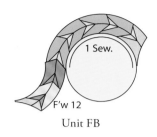

Unit FB

UNIT FC

1. Match circle C, 8 J pieces, to Freeway 9, 7 CR blocks and up to the matching point of XR block.

2. Baste circle C to Freeway 1, BR block.

3. Sew circle C, 8 J pieces, to Freeway 9, 7 CR blocks and up to the matching point of XR block.

4. Baste circle C to Freeway 1, remainder of the XR block.

5. Label this Unit FC.

Unit FC

UNIT FD

1. Sew circle D, 6 J pieces, to Freeway 11, 1 E, 3 C, and 1 F block.

2. Label this Unit FD.

Unit FD

UNIT FE

1. Sew circle E, 6 J pieces, to Freeway 17, 5 CR blocks and up to the matching point of XR block.

2. Baste circle E to Freeway 1, remainder of the XR block.

3. Label this Unit FE.

Unit FE

UNIT FF

1. Sew circle F, 6 J pieces, to Freeway 13, 4 C, and 1 F block.

2. Label this Unit FF.

Unit FF

UNIT FG

1. Sew circle G, 9 J pieces, to Freeway 5, 7 CR and 1 FR block.

2. Label this Unit FG.

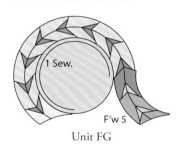

Unit FG

UNIT FH

1. Sew circle L, 9 J pieces, to Freeway 3, 7 C and 1 F block.

2. Label this Unit FH.

Unit FH

UNIT FI

1. Match circle I, 5 J pieces, to Freeway 7, 4 CR blocks and up to the matching point of the XR block.

2. Baste circle I to Freeway 7, BR block.

3. Sew circle I, 5 J pieces, to Freeway 7, 4 CR blocks, and up to the matching point of the XR block.

4. Baste circle I to Freeway 7, remainder of the XR block.

5. Label this Unit FI.

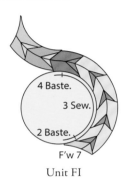

Unit FI

UNIT FJ

1. Match circle J, 8 J pieces, to Freeway 16, 7 C blocks and up to the matching point of the X block.

2. Baste circle J to Freeway 16, B block.

3. Sew circle J, 8 J pieces to, Freeway 16, 7 C blocks and up to the matching point of the X block.

4. Baste circle J to Freeway 16, remainder of the X block.

5. Label this Unit FJ.

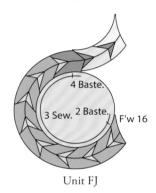

Unit FJ

UNIT FK

1. Sew circle K, 6 J pieces, to Freeway 6, 5 CR blocks and up to the matching point of the XR block.

2. Baste circle K to Freeway 16, remainder of the X block.

5. Label this Unit FK.

Unit FK

> >

Joining the Units

On a flat surface, lay out the Freeways as directed. Where there are no matching points, pin the ends, then find midpoints and quarter points. Match these, and sew them together. When joining to places that have only been basted, check that the fabrics are lying flat, without stretching or puckering, and sew the original seams securely.

Some seams will again only be basted initially. *Place 2 safety pins in basted seams to make them easy to find them again later,* and sew securely at that stage.

UNIT FL

Freeways 4 and 15 and Insert

Unit FL

1. Match Freeway 15, CR block overhang, to Freeway 4, F block short side.

2. Match the insert corner to Freeway 15 back corner.

3. Match the midpoints of the neighboring sides, and sew.

4. Label this Unit FL.

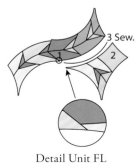

Detail Unit FL

UNIT FM

Units FH and FK

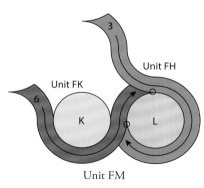

Unit FM

1. Match Freeway 3, C block overhang, to Freeway 6, F block short side.

2. Match Freeway 6, C block overhang, to Freeway 3, F block short side.

3. Sew Freeway 6, F, and C blocks, to circle L, 3 J pieces.

4. Sew Freeway 3 front to Freeway 6 outer curve.

5. Sew Freeway 6 front to Freeway 3 outer curve.

6. Label this Unit FM.

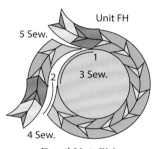

Detail Unit FM

UNIT FN

Units FL and FM

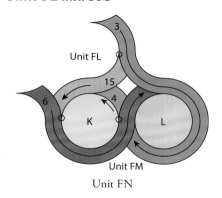

Unit FN

1. Sew Freeway 6, XR block overhang, to Freeway 4, B block short side.

2. Match the quarter points of Freeway 4 back and the insert to Freeway 6, C and F blocks. Sew.

3. Match Freeway 6, C block overhang, to Freeway 15, FR block short side.

4. Sew Freeway 6, basted XR block; Freeway 4, BR and FR blocks; and Freeway 15, FR and CR blocks to circle K, 6 J pieces.

5. Sew Freeway 15 front to Freeway 6 outer curve.

6. Match Freeway 3, X block overhang, to Freeway 15, B block short side.

7. Match the quarter points of Freeway 15 back and the insert to Freeway 3 outer curve. Sew.

8. Label this Unit FN.

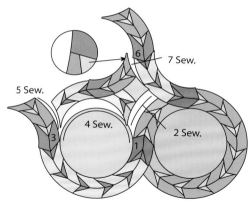

Detail Unit FN

UNIT FO

Units FJ and FN

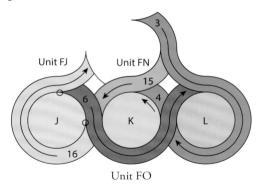

Unit FJ Unit FN

Unit FO

1. Match Freeway 16, X block overhang, to Freeway 6, B block short side.

2. Match Freeway 6, X block overhang, to Freeway 16, B block short side.

3. Match the quarter points of Freeway 16, basted X block; Freeway 6, B, C, and X blocks; and Freeway 16, basted B block, to 4 J pieces from circle J. Sew.

4. Sew Freeway 16 back to Freeway 6 outer curve.

5. Baste the insert to Freeway 15 outer curve.

6. Match the quarter points of the insert to Freeway 6, B and C blocks. Sew.

7. Match the quarter points of the insert and Freeway 6 back, to Freeway 16, FR and CR blocks. Sew.

8. Label this Unit FO.

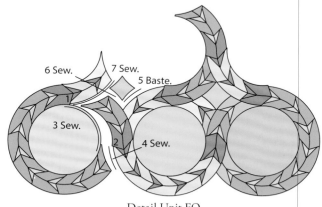

6 Sew. 7 Sew. 5 Baste.
3 Sew. 2 4 Sew.

Detail Unit FO

UNIT FP

Unit FI, Freeway 14, and Insert

1. Match Freeway 7, XR block overhang, to Freeway 14, BR block short side.

2. Match the quarter points of the insert and Freeway 14 back, to Freeway 7, F and C blocks. Sew.

3. Sew Freeway 7, basted X block, and Freeway 14, BR and FR blocks, to circle I, 3 J pieces.

4. Label this Unit FP.

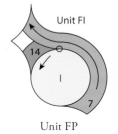

Unit FI

14 I 7

Unit FP

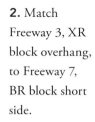

2 Sew. 3 Sew.

Detail Unit FP

UNIT FQ

Units FO and FP

1. Match Freeway 3, CR block overhang, to Freeway 14, FR block short side.

2. Match Freeway 3, XR block overhang, to Freeway 7, BR block short side.

3. Match Freeway 3, B, C, X, 2 CR, and XR blocks, and Freeway 7, basted BR block, to the insert; Freeway 14 front; and circle I, 4 J pieces. Sew.

4. Sew Freeway 7 back to Freeway 3 outer curve.

5. Label this Unit FQ.

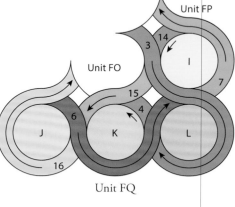

Unit FP
Unit FO
3 14 I
15 7
6 4
J K L
16

Unit FQ

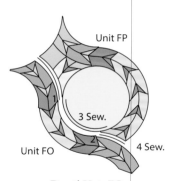

Unit FP
1
3 Sew.
Unit FO 2 4 Sew.

Detail Unit FQ

UNIT FR

Unit FE and Freeway 10

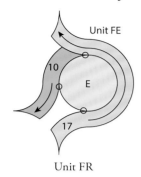

1. Match Freeway 17, XR block overhang, to Freeway 10, BR block short side.

2. Sew Freeway 10 back to Freeway 17 outer curve.

3. Sew Freeway 17, basted XR block, and Freeway 10, BR, CR, and XR blocks up to the matching point, to circle E, 3 J pieces.

4. Baste Freeway 10, XR block, to circle E.

5. Label this Unit FR.

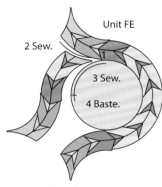

Detail Unit FR

UNIT FS

Unit FR, Freeway 2, and Insert

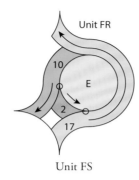

1. Match Freeway 10, XR overhang, to Freeway 2, BR block short side.

2. Match Freeway 17, CR overhang, to Freeway 2, FR block short side.

3. Sew Freeway 10, basted XR block, and Freeway 2, BR and FR blocks, to circle E, 3 J pieces.

4. Match the quarter points of Freeway 2 back, and the insert to Freeway 10, C and F blocks. Sew.

5. Match the quarter points of the insert and Freeway 2 front, to Freeway 17, B, C, and X blocks. Sew.

6. Label this Unit FS.

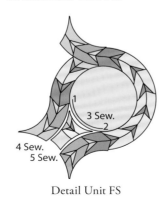

Detail Unit FS

UNIT FT

Units FG and FQ and Circle H

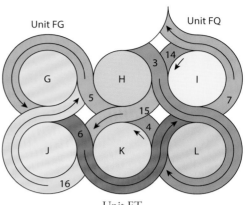

Unit FT

Circle G to Unit FQ

1. Match Freeway 5, CR block overhang, to Freeway 16, FR block. Sew short side.

2. Match the corners of Freeway 5 back, and the insert.

3. Using quarter points, sew Freeway 5, B, C, and X blocks, to the insert and Freeway 16 front.

Freeway 16 to Unit FG

4. Match Freeway 16, CR block overhang, to Freeway 5, FR block short side.

5. Sew Freeway 16, FR and CR blocks, to circle G, 3 J pieces.

6. Sew Freeway 5 front to Freeway 16 outer curve.

7. Match Freeway 15, X block overhang, to Freeway 5, B block short side.

8. Sew Freeway 5 back and basted insert, to Freeway 15, FR and CR blocks.

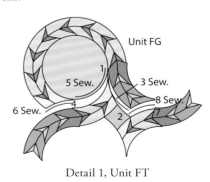

Detail 1, Unit FT

Insert Circle H

1. Match the seam between Freeway 3, B and C blocks, to a seam between circle H, 2 J pieces.

2. Baste Freeway 3, B block, to circle H.

3. Sew Freeway 3, C and X blocks; plus Freeway 15, B, C and X blocks; and Freeway 5, B, C blocks, and up to the matching point of the X block, to the next 8 J pieces in circle H.

4. Baste circle H to Freeway 5, remainder of the X block.

5. Label this Unit FT.

Detail 2, Unit FT

UNIT FU

Unit FS and FT

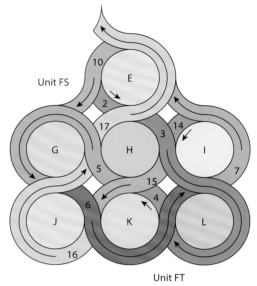

Unit FS

Unit FT

Unit FU

1. Match Freeway 5, X block overhang, to Freeway 17, B block short side.

2. Baste Freeway 17 back, the insert, and Freeway 10 front to Freeway 5 outer curve.

3. Match Freeway 17, X block overhang, to Freeway 3, B block short side.

4. Sew Freeway 5, basted X block, plus Freeway 17, B, C, and X blocks, and Freeway 3, B block to circle H, 4 J pieces, to complete the circle.

5. Baste Freeway 3 back, the insert, and Freeway 7 front to Freeway 17 outer curve.

6. Label this Unit FU.

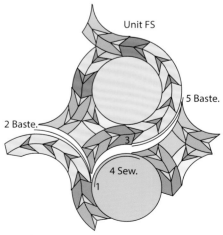

Detail Unit FU

UNIT FV

Unit FF and Freeway 8

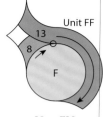

Unit FV

1. Match Freeway 13, C block overhang to Freeway 8, F block short side.

2. Match the quarter points of the insert and Freeway 8 front, to Freeway 13, BR, CR, and XR blocks. Sew.

3. Sew Freeway 8, F and E blocks, to circle F, 3 J pieces.

4. Label this Unit FV.

Detail Unit FV

UNIT FW

Units FC and FV

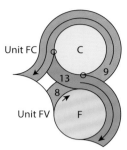

Unit FW

1. Match Freeway 9, XR block overhang, to Freeway 13, BR block short side.

2. Match the quarter points of the insert and Freeway 13 back, to Freeway 9, F and C blocks. Sew.

3. Match Freeway 13, block XR overhang, to Freeway 9, BR block short side.

4. Sew Freeway 9, basted X; Freeway 13, BR, CR, and XR blocks; and Freeway 9, basted BR block, to circle C, 4 J pieces.

5. Sew Freeway 9 back to Freeway 13 outer curve.

6. Label this Unit FW.

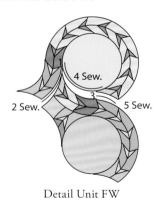

Detail Unit FW

UNIT FX

Units FB and FA

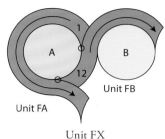

Unit FX

1. Match Freeway 1, XR block overhang, to Freeway 12, BR block short side.

2. Match Freeway 12, XR block overhang, to Freeway 1, BR block short side.

3. Sew Freeway 1, basted XR block; Freeway 12, BR, CR, and XR blocks; and Freeway 1, BR block, to circle A, 4 J pieces.

4. Sew Freeway 1 back to Freeway 12 outer curve.

5. Sew Freeway 12 back to Freeway 1 outer curve.

6. Label this Unit FX.

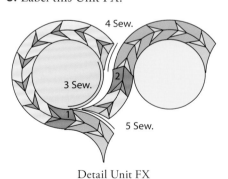

Detail Unit FX

UNIT FY

Units FW and FX

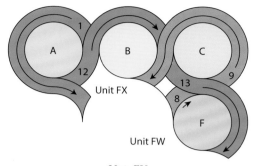

Unit FY

1. Match Freeway 9, C block overhang, to Freeway 12, F block short side.

2. Sew Freeway 9, C and F blocks, to circle B, 3 J pieces.

3. Sew Freeway 12 front to Freeway 9 outer curve.

4. Label this Unit FY.

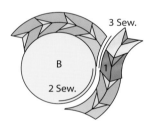

Detail Unit FY

UNIT FZ

Units FD and FY

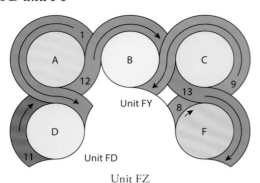

Unit FY

Unit FD

Unit FZ

1. Match Freeway 1, C block overhang, to Freeway 11, F block short side.

2. Sew Freeway 1, C, and F blocks, to circle D, 3 J pieces.

3. Sew Freeway 11 front to Freeway 1 outer curve.

4. Label this Unit FZ.

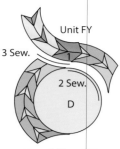

Detail Unit FZ

Quilt Center

UNITS FU AND FZ

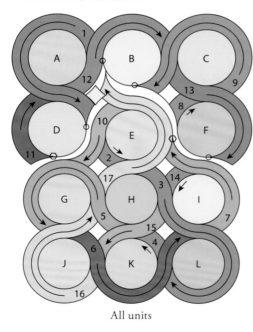

All units

Freeway 17

1. Match Freeway 12, C block overhang, to Freeway 17, F block short side.

2. Match Freeway 17, C block overhang, to Freeway 9, F block short side.

3. Sew Freeway 17, F and C blocks, to circle B, 3 J pieces.

4. Match Freeway 8, E block short side, to Freeway 7, F block short side.

5. Match the quarter points of Freeway 9 front, the insert, and Freeway 8 back to Freeway 17 outer edge. Sew.

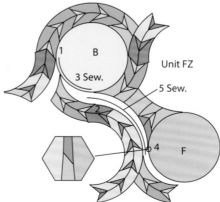

Detail 1, Quilt Center

Freeway 7

6. Match Freeway 7, C block overhang, to Freeway 13, F block short side.

7. Sew Freeway 7, F and C blocks, to circle F, 3 J pieces.

8. Sew Freeway 13 front to Freeway 7 outer curve.

9. Baste Freeway 7 front to Freeway 17 outer curve.

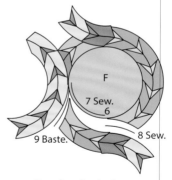

Detail 2, Quilt Center

Insert

For the following, note that seams do not meet at the corner.

10. Pin the insert to Freeway 12.

11. Sew the insert to Freeway 1 and Freeway 12.

12. Baste the insert to Freeway 17.

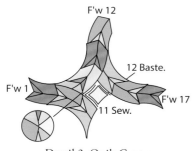

Detail 3, Quilt Center

Freeway 10 and Freeway 5

13. Match Freeway 17, XR block overhang, to Freeway 10, BR block short side.

14. Match the quarter points of the insert and Freeway 10 back, to Freeway 17, F and C blocks. Sew.

15. Match Freeway 10, C block overhang, to Freeway 1, F block short side.

16. Match the quarter points of the insert and Freeway 1 front, to Freeway 10, BR, CR, and XR blocks. Sew.

17. Match Freeway 10, F block short side, to Freeway 11, E block short side.

18. Sew Freeway 10, C and F blocks, to circle D, 3 J pieces.

19. Baste Freeway 11 back to Freeway 5 outer curve.

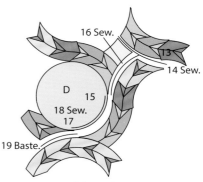

Detail 4, Quilt Center

20. Lay your quilt top on a flat surface, and check for any safety pin markers indicating basted seams. Sew these seams securely.

Borders

BACKGROUND BORDER

Patterns

Refer to Preparing the Background Border Patterns (page 16).

1. Cut a rectangle of freezer paper 9″ × 75″.

2. Draw a line with a ruler ½″ from a long edge.

3. Draw a 3-circle border following directions (page 16).

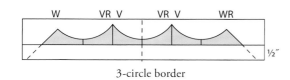

3-circle border

4. Cut a rectangle of freezer paper 9″ × 95″.

5. Draw a line with a ruler ½″ from a long edge.

6. Draw a 4-circle border following directions (page 17).

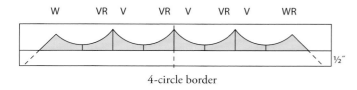

4-circle border

CUTTING

Refer to Marking the Background Border (page 17).

Starch and press all fabric before cutting to minimize stretching.

1. Press the 4-circle freezer-paper template to the wrong side of the fabric rectangle. Trace around the template. The dashed line is the sewing line. The solid line is the cutting line.

2. Leaving at least ½″ between the sewing lines, trace around the 4 border freezer-paper template again.

3. Repeat with the 3-circle-border freezer-paper template twice.

4. Cut ¼″ from the sewing line of the borders when ready to sew.

ADDING THE BACKGROUND BORDER

Refer to Attaching the Background Border (page 18).

Finishing the Quilt

1. Cut the backing fabric into 2 equal lengths.

2. Refer to Finishing (page 19).

Quilting

This quilt was free-motion ditch quilted throughout. The spine of the Freeways was ditch stitched first, and then 2 more rows of quilting were added on either side of this line. The circle wedges had 3 extra arcs added to each wedge, and the border was echo quilted around the curves to the edge of the quilt approximately ½″ apart.

PREPARING THE QUILT FOR BINDING

Due to having so many curves and bias edges, particularly in the border, extra care needs to be taken to ensure the quilt is flat.

1. Using 2 or more long rulers, draw a line on the right side of the quilt at the place you think will be the edge of your finished quilt. This line needs to be the same distance from the outer edge of the Freeways on all sides.

2. Place a pin at the middle of the corner circle. Measuring from that point to the edge of the quilt, draw a quarter circle around the corner.

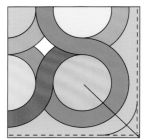

Draw curve on corners.

3. Using the longest stitch on your machine, stitch these lines in a thread color that is easily seen.

4. *Don't* trim the extra fabric from the sides or corners until *after the binding has been sewn on.*

5. Measure the quilt to ensure the sides are the same length as the length through the middle of the quilt.

6. If they differ, determine the average of the lengths to find your target length.

•----------- Adjusting a Side Length -----------•

1. Working on the back of your quilt and using a different thread color, sew 2 basting rows along the straight sections of the quilt edge, 1 just outside the stitched line and another ½″ further in.

2. Leave a tail of thread at both ends of these stitching lines on each border. Tie the thread ends together on the back of the quilt.

3. On the top side of the quilt, pull the thread up slightly on one end, and tie the ends together. Carefully pull up the loose threads to bring the quilt into the required size.

4. Gently spread the excess bulk throughout the entire side. The quilt sides should now be the same length as the middle of the quilt.

Binding the Quilt

As the corners are curved, bias binding is needed rather than straight-cut binding for the corner sections. *Freeways* uses 12″ leftover strips from the quilt and 1 fat quarter for the binding.

Continuous Bias Binding

As the outer edge has curved corners, it is necessary to cut the binding for this on the bias. Binding cut along the straight grain of the fabric will neither sit flat nor bend around the curves. The following method generates a long, continuous strip of bias binding. Take care when pressing and sewing to not stretch the fabric. Starch and press the fabric before beginning.

1. Trim the fat quarter to be a square.

2. Label 2 opposite sides of the fat quarter A and B, and cut diagonally.

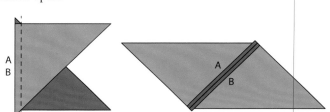

Label and cut.

3. Using a slightly shorter stitch length, with right sides facing, ends offset ¼″, and matching the labeled sides, sew together. Press seams open.

Stitch and press seam open.

4. On the reverse of the fabric, draw a line with a ruler ¼″ from the top edge. Rule parallel lines across the fabric at 2½″ intervals.

5. Label the lines as shown.

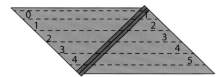

Draw and label lines.

6. Fold the fabric right sides together, aligning the raw numbered edges and carefully matching the numbers 1 to 1,

2 to 2, and so forth. Pin to secure, forming a tube. Note that neither 0 nor the highest number are matched.

Match numbers, pin, and stitch.

7. Using a ¼″ seam and a slightly shorter stitch, machine stitch the pinned seam. Press the seam open. It is necessary to rotate the tube to press the seam.

8. Using fabric scissors, cut along the ruled line, spiraling around the tube.

Cut along marked line.

9. Taking great care not to stretch the strip, press the binding in half lengthwise with the wrong sides together.

10. Cut into 4 equal strips approximately 30″ long, one for each corner.

BINDING THE QUILT

1. Using the 2½″ × 12″ scrap strips, refer to Binding (page 19), and join all of the strips.

2. Measure the quilt length, and cut 1 strip 27½″ less than this length. This is Strip C.

3. Measure the quilt width, and cut 2 strips 27½″ less than this width for strips B and D.

4. Cut 2 strips, each ½ of the measured length. These are strips A and E.

5. Using 45° seams, sew the strips end to end, alternating a bias strip with each scrap strip: strip A, bias, strip B, bias, strip C, bias, strip D, bias, strip E.

6. Lay this on the quilt to check that it fits, and adjust if needed.

7. Refer to Binding (page 19) to complete, starting and finishing near the middle of a long side.

8. Label your quilt.

Measure quilt.

Alternate Path Color Option

MATERIALS

One-colored path version

Fabric 1: 5 yards for all Freeways

16 assorted fabrics: 1¾″ strips for arrows or scraps

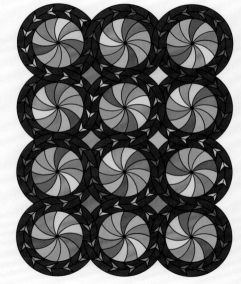

MATERIALS

Alternate multicolored version; use your own fabrics in the various paths

Fabric 1: ⅔ yard for Freeway 3

Fabrics 2–7: ½ yard each for Freeways 1, 5, 6, 9, 16, and 17

Fabrics 8–10: ⅓ yard each for Freeways 7, 12, and 13

Fabrics 11–13: ⅓ yard each for Freeways 10, 11, and 15

Fabrics 14–17: fat sixteenth of each for Freeways 2, 4, 14, and 8

Arrows may be cut from path and wedge fabrics

Tracks

FINISHED CIRCLE
16" diameter

DESIGN AREA
46" × 66½"

FINISHED TRACKS
4½" wide

FINISHED QUILT
65" × 85½"

ELEMENTS: 3-circle foundation-pieced-wedge layout, one-color clockwise and counter-clockwise paths, background border, straight border, free-motion machine quilting

By Cinzia White

Terminology

To understand the abbreviations and construction it is important that the Blocks and Terminology (page 13) is read first, paying particular attention to The Blocks (page 13) and Overview of Path Formation (page 14).

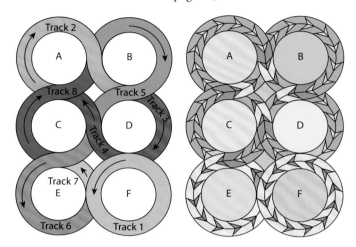

⚙ Note

- The paths are constructed using a combination of 5 basic blocks and 3 variations. Information about the basic blocks is provided in Block Construction (page 14).

- The variations affect some of the front and back blocks only. They are D (different front), E (extended back), and H (huge back) which move in a clockwise direction, or DR (different front reversed), ER (extended back reversed), and HR (huge back reversed) which travel in a counter-clockwise direction.

- Paths are broken when crossing under other paths and continue again in a variety of ways. This creates a number of variations for the Front/Front Reversed and the Back/Back Reversed blocks.

- Comparing the variation blocks it may be seen that the blocks are identical except that 1 template is extended or shortened slightly when approaching the short side.

CLOCKWISE BLOCKS

- Block D (different front) uses 1 piece using template M and 1 piece using template Y from the same fabric and 1 contrasting block A.

- Block E (extended back) uses 1 piece using template S and 1 piece using template U from the same fabric.

- Block H (huge back) uses 1 piece using template S and 1 piece template X from the same fabric.

COUNTER-CLOCKWISE BLOCKS

- Block DR (different front reversed) uses 1 piece using template MR and 1 piece using template YR from the same fabric and 1 contrasting block AR.

- Block ER (extended back reversed) uses 1 piece using template SR and 1 piece using template UR from the same fabric.

- Block HR (huge back reversed) uses 1 piece using template SR and 1 piece using template XR from the same fabric.

The variations are dependent on how the blocks meet and crossover.

1. Both paths are heading in the same direction. This is the most common crossover and uses block B/BR and block FR/F. These points are marked with circles.

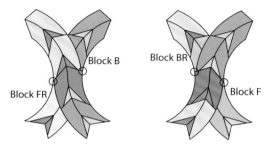

Paths going in same direction

2. The paths are heading in opposite directions. This uses block H/HR and block DR/D and the points are marked with stars.

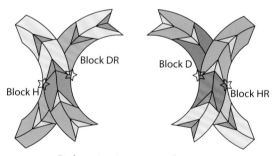

Paths going in opposite directions

3. The paths don't cross. This uses block E/ER and block F/FR and the points are marked with hexagons.

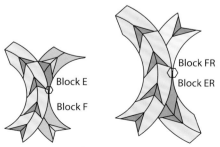

Paths not crossing

BACK BLOCK COMPARISONS

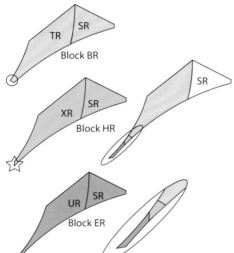

S
T
Block B

S
X
Block H

S
U
Block E

S

Clockwise variations

TR
SR
Block BR

XR
SR
Block HR

SR

UR
SR
Block ER

Counter-clockwise variations

FRONT BLOCK COMPARISONS

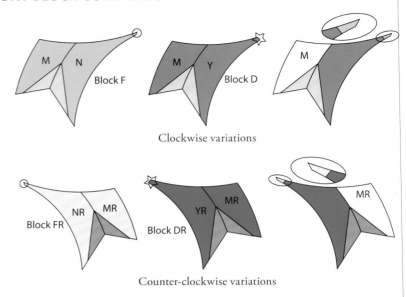

M
N
Block F

M
Y
Block D

M

Clockwise variations

NR
MR
Block FR

YR
MR
Block DR

MR

Counter-clockwise variations

Tips

- When making *Trails or Tracks* it is easiest to cut the front and back blocks from the largest template, mark the correct seam line, and then cut down to the correct size when joining the paths. If doing this *initially cut all front blocks using template N or NR and back blocks using template U or UR.*

- Work sequentially, following the paths, starting with the easiest construction requirements.

- Number each path as per the layout design. Do not remove the numbers until you have sewn the complete quilt top together. It is extremely difficult to work out the layout of the paths without the numbers.

- All measurements include ¼″ seam allowance.

- All fabric is cut across the width of the fabric using templates unless otherwise stated.

- I recommend that you make a sample path and 1 circle before cutting out all of the pieces to complete the quilt.

- All templates show both the sewing line, marked with a dashed line, and the cutting line, marked with a solid line.

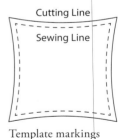

Cutting Line

Sewing Line

Template markings

TEMPLATES

Make templates for:

- K and L for block A and AR
- S and T for block B
- O and P for block C and CR
- M and Y for block DR
- S and U for block E and ER
- M and N for block F and FR
- S and X for block H
- Q and R for block X
- I for insert
- J for the circle wedges (optional)

MATERIALS

Refer to Supplies and Tools (page 7).

Fabric amounts are based on 40″ width of fabric.

Dark grey print: 5½ yards for Tracks and outer border 2

Peacock Print: 4 yards for the arrows, circles, inserts, Border 1, and binding. More fabric may be needed if fussy cutting.

Backing: 5⅛ yards

Batting: 71″ × 92″

●------- **Fussy Cutting** -------●

If you are planning to fussy cut the fabric, cut patterns for the circle and border from freezer paper. Take these when shopping for the fabric and place them on the fabric to determine the amount needed.

●----------------------------●

SUPPLIES AND TOOLS

See General Information; Supplies and Tools (page 7).

Freezer paper, 18″-wide: 2⅓ yards

CUTTING

Starch and press all fabric before cutting to minimize stretching.

Always mark the center spine with an arrow; it is marked with a double-ended arrow on the template. Refer to The Blocks (page 13) for more information.

Dark Grey Print

- Cut 12 CR blocks for Track 1.
- Cut 1 H block, 7 C block, 1 X block, 1 CR block, and 1 DR block for Track 2.
- Cut 1 H block, 3 C blocks, and 1 F block for Track 3.
- Cut 1 E block, 1 C block, 1 X block, 1 CR block, and 1 DR block for Track 4.
- Cut 1 H block, 7 C blocks, 1 X block, 1 CR block, and 1 DR block for Track 5.
- Cut 1 H block, 1 C block, 1 X block, 7 CR block, and 1 FR block for Track 6.
- Cut 1 ER block and 1 FR block for Track 7.

- Cut 1 B block, 4 C block, 1 X block, 1 CR block, and 1 DR block for Track 8.
- Cut 7 rectangles 5½″ × WOF for border 2.
- Cut 1 strip 2½″ × WOF for binding.

Peacock print

Refer to Preparing the Circle Pattern (page 10) to make the circle template.

- Cut 6 circles using the prepared template.
- Cut 29 A blocks and 29 AR blocks using templates.
- Cut 2 pieces I for the inserts.
- Cut 9 strips 2½″ × WOF for binding.

Elements of the Design

TRACKS

Track 1

1. Refer to Block Construction (page 14).

2. Layout the fabric pieces for 12 CR blocks in order.

3. Sew the arrows to a neighboring unit.

4. Working from the back, join the units of 1 side first then the other.

Track 1

5. Sew the 2 halves together to complete Track 1. *If the track spine doesn't match up, check the orientation of template K/KR first. An error is easily made with this piece.*

Track 7

1. Layout the fabric pieces for 1 ER block and 1 FR block in order.

2. Referring to Block Construction (page 14) complete Track 7.

Track 7

Track 3

1. Layout the fabric pieces for 1 H block, 3 C blocks, and 1 F block in order.

2. Referring to Block Construction, Counterclockwise Blocks (page 15) complete Track 3.

Track 3

Track 4

1. Layout the fabric pieces for 1 E block, 1 C block, 1 X block, 1 CR block, and 1 DR block in order.

2. Referring to Block Construction, Counterclockwise Blocks (page 15) complete Track 4.

Track 4

Track 2

1. Layout the fabric pieces for 1 H block, 7 C blocks, 1 X block, 1 CR block, and 1 DR block in order.

2. Referring to Block Construction, Counterclockwise Blocks (page 15) complete Track 2. Note that the center spine must always line up, but the outer edges between block X and block CR do not line up.

3. Make 2 for Tracks 2 and 5.

Track 2

Track 8

1. Layout the fabric pieces for 1 B block, 4 C blocks, 1 X block, 1 CR block, and 1 DR block in order.

2. Referring to Block Construction, Counterclockwise Blocks (page 15) complete Track 8.

Track 8

Track 6

1. Layout the fabric pieces for 1 H block, 1 C block, 1 X block, 7 CR blocks, and 1 FR block in order.

2. Referring to Block Construction, Counterclockwise Blocks (page 15) complete Track 6.

Track 6

CIRCLES

If you are using pieced circles, refer to Making the Circles (page 10) and make 6 circles. Make sure they are sized correctly and redraw the outer sewing/cutting line if necessary. If you are using fussy cut circles, mark the matching points as noted in Preparing the Circle Pattern (page 10).

Place the circles in the quilt and label. Refer to Checking the Circle Fit (page 15).

JOINING TRACKS AND CIRCLES

Refer to Joining Paths and Circles, and Joining Crossover Blocks to Circle (page 15).

Some seams are initially basted as there is only 1 definite matching point. Place 2 safety pins in these seams to make it easy to find them again later.

Later when joining to places that have only been basted sew the original seams securely.

Units KA and KB

1. Match marked circle A (or 8 J pieces) to Track 2, 7 C blocks, and up to the matching point of the X block.

2. Baste circle A to Track 8, H block.

3. Sew circle A to Track 2, 7 C blocks, and up to the matching point of the X block.

4. Baste circle A to Track 2, the remainder of the X block.

5. Label this Unit KA.

Unit KA

6. Repeat with circle B and Track 5.

7. Label this Unit KB.

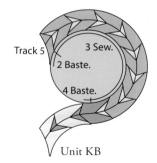

Unit KB

Unit KC

1. Match marked circle C (or 5 J pieces) to Track 8, 4 C blocks, and up to the matching point of the X block.

2. Baste circle C to Track 8, B block.

3. Sew circle C to Track 8, 4 C blocks, and up to the matching point of the X block.

4. Baste circle C to Track 8, the remainder of the X block.

5. Label this Unit KC.

Unit KC

Unit KD

1. Sew marked circle D (or 5 J pieces) to Track 3, 3 C, and 1 F blocks.

2. Match the quarter points of circle D to Track 4, 1 E, 1 C blocks, and up to the matching point of the X block. Sew.

3. Baste circle D to Track 4, the remainder of the X block.

4. Label this Unit KD.

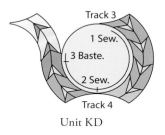

Unit KD

Unit KE

1. Sew marked circle E (or 9 J pieces) to Track 6, 7 CR, and I FR blocks.

2. Label this Unit KE.

Unit KE

Unit KF

1. Sew marked circle F (or 12 J pieces) to Track 1, 12 CR blocks.

2. Label this Unit KF.

Unit KF

Unit KG

1. Sew Track 7, 1 ER, and 1 FR blocks to 1 I piece.

2. Label this Unit KG.

Unit KG

JOINING THE UNITS

On a flat surface, lay out the Trails as directed. Where there are no matching points, pin the ends then find the midpoints and quarter points. Match these and sew them together. When joining to places that have only been basted, be sure the fabrics are lying flat, without stretching or puckering, and sew the original seams securely.

Some seams will only be basted initially. *Place 2 safety pins in these seams to make it easy to find them again later* and sew securely at that stage.

Unit KH

Units KA and KB

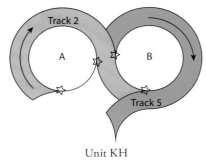

Unit KH

1. Match Track 5, X block overhang to Track 2, DR block short side.

2. Match Track 2, CR block overhang to Track 5, H block short side.

3. Match the quarter points of Track 5, basted X block, Track 2, DR and CR blocks, and Track 5, H block to circle B, 4 J pieces. Sew.

4. Sew Track 5 back to Track 2 outer curve.

5. Sew Track 2 front to Track 5 outer curve.

6. Label this Unit KH.

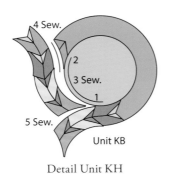

Detail Unit KH

Unit KI

Units KC and KH

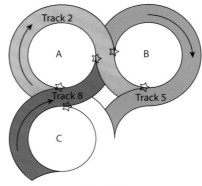

Unit KI

1. Match Track 2, X block overhang to Track 8, DR block short side.

2. Match Track 8, CR block overhang to Track 2, H block short side.

3. Match the quarter points of Track 2, basted X block, Track 8, DR and CR blocks, and Track 2, H block to circle A. Sew.

4. Sew Track 2 back to Track 8 outer curve.

Detail 1, Unit KI

5. Baste the insert to Track 8 outer curve. The insert is not the same length as the F block.

6. Match the insert corner to Track 5 front corner.

7. Match the quarter points of the insert and basted Track 2 front to Track 5, CR, and DR blocks. Sew.

8. Match the quarter points of the insert and Track 8 front to Track 2, CR, and DR blocks. Sew.

9. Label this Unit KI.

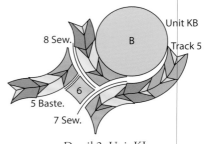

Detail 2, Unit KI

Unit KJ

Units KE and KG

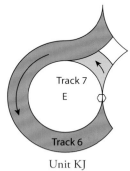

Unit KJ

1. Match Track 6, CR block overhang to Track 7, FR block short side.

2. Match Track 6, FR block short side to Track 7, ER block short side.

3. Sew Track 7, FR, and ER blocks to circle E, 3 J pieces.

4. Match the insert corner to Track 6 back corner.

5. Match the quarter points of Track 7 front and the insert to Track 6, X, C, and H blocks. Sew.

6. Label this Unit KJ.

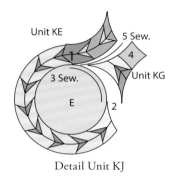

Detail Unit KJ

Unit KK

Units KD and KJ

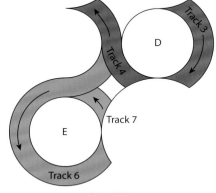

Unit KK

1. Match Track 4, CR block overhang to Track 6, H block short side.

2. Match the insert corner to Track 4 back corner.

3. Match the quarter points of Track 6 back and the insert to Track 4, X, C, and E blocks. Sew.

4. Label this Unit KK.

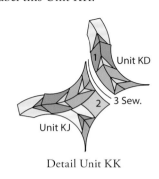

Detail Unit KK

Unit KL

Units KF and KK

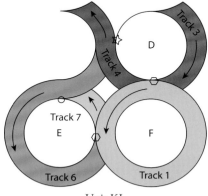

Unit KL

1. Place a pin on the inner curve line, at the point where a C block joins the neighboring C block. See detail.

2. Repeat this at every 3rd seam working around circle F.

3. Place a 24″ ruler vertically across Unit KF so that it passes through 2 opposite pin marks.

4. Place a pin on the outer edge of the path at point A.

5. Place the 24″ ruler horizontally across Unit KF, so it passes through 2 opposite pin marks.

6. Place a pin on the outer edge of the path at point B.

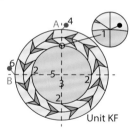

Detail 1, Unit KL

7. Using a chalk marker, draw a horizontal line going from Track 4, CR block, outer arrow back point to Track 3, C block, inner arrow back point. Pin-mark the center of the circle.

8. Draw a vertical line through the marked center. Place a pin on the outer edge of Track 4, E block where this line crosses it, at point C. This is *not* where Track 3 and Track 4 meet.

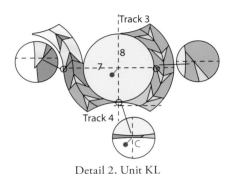

Detail 2, Unit KL

9. In Track 6 place a pin at the inner back arrow point where CR block meets the X block. See detail.

10. Repeat this at the next 2 3rd seams working around circle E.

11. Place a 24″ ruler vertically across Unit KF, so it passes through the 2 opposite pin marks.

12. Place a pin at the center of circle E.

13. Draw a horizontal line through the marked center. Place a pin on the outer edge of Track 7, E block where this line crosses it, at point D. This is NOT where Track 6 and Track 7 meet.

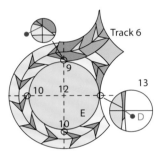

Detail 3, Unit KL

14. Match point A to point C and point B to point D.

15. Baste Track 3 front to Track 1.

16. Match the quarter points between the pins, Track 1 to Track 4 back, the insert and Track 7 back. Sew.

17. Baste Track 6 front to Track 1.

18. Label this Unit KL.

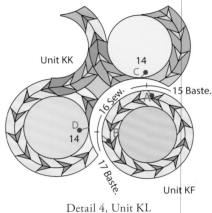

Detail 4, Unit KL

Quilt Center

Units KI and KL

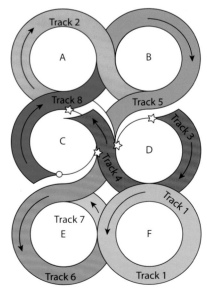

Completed center

1. Match Track 8, X block overhang to Track 4, DR block short side.

2. Match Track 6, X block overhang to Track 8, B block short side.

3. Match the quarter points of Track 8, basted X block, Track 4, FR, and CR blocks, Track 6, H, C, and X blocks, and Track 8, B block to circle C, 7 J pieces. Sew.

4. Match the insert corner to Track 4 front corner.

5. Match the quarter points of the insert and Track 4 front to Track 8, DR, and CR blocks. Sew.

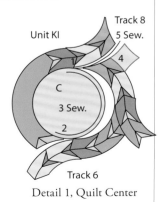

Detail 1, Quilt Center

6. Match the insert corner to Track 4 front corner.

7. Match Track 4, X block overhang to Track 5, DR block short side.

8. Match the quarter points of Track 5 front and the insert to Track 4, CR, and DR blocks. Sew.

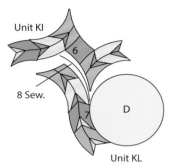

Detail 2, Quilt Center

9. Match Track 4, X block overhang to Track 5, DR block short side.

10. Match Track 5, CR block overhang to Track 3, H block short side.

11. Match the quarter points of Track 3, H block, Track 5, CR and DR blocks, and Track 4, basted X block to circle D, 5 J pieces. Sew.

12. Sew Track 3 back to Track 5 outer curve.

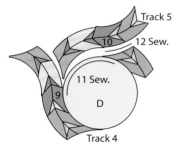

Detail 3, Quilt Center

13. Lay your quilt top on a flat surface and check for any safety pin markers indicating basted seams. Sew these seams securely.

Celebrate!

Borders

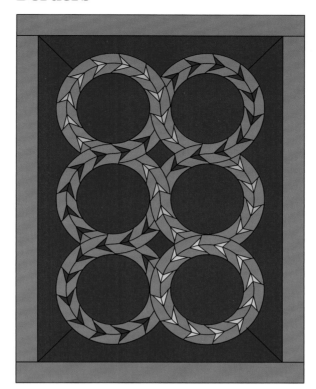

BACKGROUND BORDER

Patterns

Refer to Preparing the Background Border Patterns (page 16).

1. Cut a rectangle of freezer paper 10″ × 57″.

2. Draw a line with a ruler 2½″ from a long edge.

3. Draw a 2-circle border following directions (page 16).

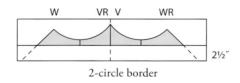

2-circle border

4. Cut a rectangle of freezer paper 10″ × 80″.

5. Draw a line with a ruler 2½″ from a long edge.

6. Draw a 3-circle border following directions (page 16).

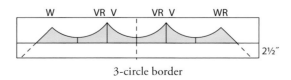

3-circle border

PEACOCK FABRIC

1. Press the 3-circle border freezer-paper template to the wrong side of the fabric rectangle. Trace around the template. The dashed line is the sewing line. The solid line is the cutting line.

2. Leaving at least ½″ between the sewing lines trace around the 3 border freezer-paper template again.

3. Repeat with the 2-circle border freezer-paper template twice.

4. Cut ¼″ from the sewing line of the borders when ready to sew.

BACKGROUND BORDER

Refer to Attaching the Background Border (page 18).

BORDER 2

1. Join all 5½″ border rectangles together end-to-end into 1 long rectangle.

2. Measure the quilt top through the center lengthwise. This was 75½″.

3. Add 1″ to this measurement and cut 2 border rectangles to this measurement. Place a pin ½″ from both ends, in the middle of the rectangle and ½ way between each of the other pins. The rectangle is pinned at quarter points ignoring the ½″ at both ends.

4. Pin-mark the sides of the quilt top in quarters.

5. Pin the borders to the quilt top, matching the pin-marks, and stitch into place.

6. Press the seams outward.

7. Trim the border level with the quilt top.

8. Measure the quilt top through the center widthwise. This was 65″.

9. Add 1″ to this measurement and cut 2 border rectangles to this measurement plus 1″.

10. Repeat Steps 4–7 to add borders to the short sides.

Finishing the Quilt

1. Cut the backing fabric into 2 equal lengths.

2. Refer to Finishing (page 19).

Quilting

This quilt was free-motion quilted around the features of the fabric. Stippling filled the background areas. The arrows in the Tracks were ditch stitched and then the center spine was echoed at ½″ intervals, 3 times on both sides. The border is filled with a ruler-quilted wavy zigzag design.

Binding the Quilt

Using the 2½″ strips refer to Binding (page 19).

Multicolored Version

MATERIALS

Fabrics 1–3: ½ yard each for Tracks 1, 2 and 5

Fabric 4: ¼ yard for Track 7

Fabrics 5–6: ⅓ yard each for Tracks 3 and 4

Fabric 7: fat sixteenth for Track 6

Fabrics 8–16: fat quarter of each for the circle wedges and inserts

Trails

FINISHED CIRCLE
16″ diameter

DESIGN AREA
107″ × 107″

FINISHED TRAIL
4½″ wide

FINISHED QUILT
120½″ × 120½″

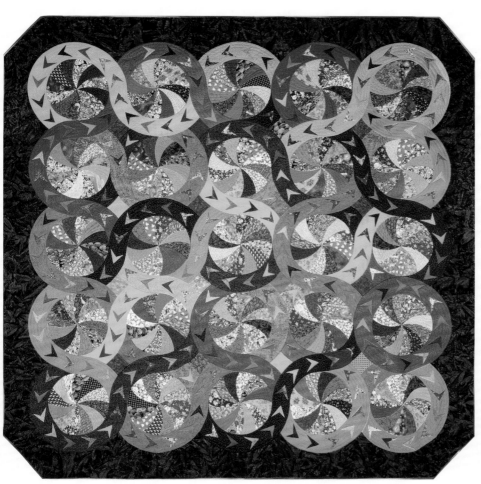

By Cinzia White

Photo by: Anthony Burns, Homepix Photography

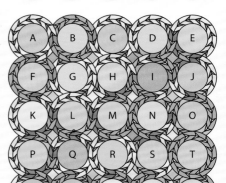

Terminology

To understand the abbreviations and construction, it is important that you read Preparing the Templates (page 7), The Blocks (page 13), Overview of Path Formation (page 14), and *Tracks,* Terminology (page 51).

TEMPLATES

Make templates for:

- K and L for blocks A and AR
- S and T for blocks B and BR
- O and P for blocks C and CR
- M and Y for blocks D and DR
- S and U for blocks E and ER

- M and N for blocks F and FR
- S and X for blocks H and HR
- Q and R for blocks X and XR
- I for insert
- J for the circle wedges

MATERIALS

Refer to Supplies and Tools (page 7).

Fabric amounts are based on 42" width of fabric.

Violet-red print: 1⅔ yard for Trails 1, 9, 20, and 30

Olive print: 1⅔ yards for Trails 2, 18, 22, 36, and 39

Vibrant aqua print: ⅓ yard for Trail 3

Orange print: 1⅓ yards for Trails 4, 8, 17, and 26

Red print: ⅔ yard for Trails 5, 31, and 40

Pale purple print: fat sixteenth for Trail 6

Yellow print: 1½ yard for Trails 7, 14, 27, and 34

Purple on black print: ⅔ yard for Trails 10 and 38

Green on black print: fat sixteenth for Trail 11

Dark green print: 1¼ yards for Trails 12, 16, 21, and 32

Pink on black print: 1¼ yards for Trails 13, 15, 28, and 37

Aqua print: 1¼ yards for Trails 19, 23, 25, 35, and 41

Lime-green print: 1¼ yards for Trails 24, 29, and 33

40 assorted fabrics: ¼ yard each for the circle wedges and inserts

Purple batik: 3⅓ yards for border

Backing: 10½ yards

Batting: 126" × 126"

Multicolored print: 1 yard for binding

No extra fabric needs to be purchased for the arrows (blocks A and AR). These are cut from fabric remaining after cutting out the Trails, inserts, and circle wedges.

SUPPLIES AND TOOLS

See General Information; Supplies and Tools (page 7).

Freezer paper, 18"-wide: 3½ yards

CUTTING

Starch and press all fabric before cutting to minimize stretching.

Always mark the center spine with an arrow; it is marked with a double-ended arrow on the template. Refer to The Blocks (page 13) for more information.

Violet-red print

- Cut 12 C blocks for Trail 1.
- Cut 1 HR block, 6 CR blocks, and 1 DR block for Trail 9.
- Cut 1 ER block, 4 CR blocks, 1 XR block, 1 C block, and 1 D block for Trail 20.
- Cut 1 HR block, 1 CR block, 1 XR block, 5 C blocks, 1 X block, 1 CR block, and 1 FR block for Trail 30.

Olive print

- Cut 1 E block and 1 F block for Trail 2.
- Cut 1 HR block, 4 CR block, 1 XR block, 1 C block, and 1 F block for Trail 18.
- Cut 1 ER block, 1 CR block, 1 XR block, 5 C blocks, 1 X block, 1 CR block, and 1 DR block for Trail 22.
- Cut 1 ER block, 3 CR blocks, and 1 FR block for Trail 36.
- Cut 1 BR block, 4 CR blocks, 1 XR block, 1 C block, and 1 F block for Trail 39.

Vibrant aqua print

- Cut 1 E block, 6 C blocks, and 1 F block for Trail 3.

Orange print

- Cut 1 HR block, 6 CR blocks, and 1 DR block for Trail 4.

- Cut 1 BR block, 4 CR blocks, 1 XR block, 1 C block, and 1 D block for Trail 8.

- Cut 1 HR block, 4 CR blocks, 1 XR block, 1 C block, and 1 D block for Trail 17.

- Cut 1 HR block, 1 CR block, 1 XR block, 1 C block, and 1 F block for Trail 26.

Red print

- Cut 1 H block and 1 F block for Trail 5.

- Cut 1 B block, 4 C blocks, 1 X block, 1 CR block, and 1 FR block for Trail 31.

- Cut 1 BR block and 1 FR block for Trail 40.

Pale purple print

- Cut 1 B block and 1 D block for Trail 6.

Yellow print

- Cut 1 HR block, 1 CR block, 1 XR block, 1 C block, and 1 F block for Trail 7.

- Cut 1 ER block, 1 CR block, 1 XR block, 1 C block, and 1 F block for Trail 14.

- Cut 1 BR block, 1 CR block, 1 XR block, 1 C block, and 1 D block for Trail 27.

- Cut 1 B block, 4 C blocks, 1 X block, 7 CR blocks, and 1 FR block for Trail 34.

Purple on black print

- Cut 1 H block, 1 C block, 1 X block, 2 CR blocks, 1 XR block, 4 C blocks, and 1 F block for Trail 10.

- Cut 1 B block and 1 F block for Trail 38.

Green on black print

- Cut 1 E block and 1 F block for Trail 11.

Dark green print

- Cut 1 BR block and 1 DR block for Trail 12.

- Cut 1 HR block, 4 CR blocks, 1 XR block, 1 C block, and 1 D block for Trail 16.

- Cut 1 HR block, 4 CR blocks, 1 XR block, 2 C blocks, 1 X block, 1 CR block, and 1 FR block for Trail 21.

- Cut 1 ER block and 1 FR block for Trail 32.

Pink on black print

- Cut 1 H block, 1 C block, 1 X block, 4 CR blocks, and 1 FR block for Trail 13.

- Cut 1 E block, 3 C blocks, and 1 D block for Trail 15.

- Cut 1 HR block, 7 CR blocks, 1 XR block, 2 C blocks, 1 X block, 1 CR block, and 1 FR block for Trail 28.

- Cut 1 ER block and 1 FR block for Trail 37.

Aqua print

- Cut 1 BR block, 3 CR blocks, and 1 FR block for Trail 19.

- Cut 1 H block and 1 D block for Trail 23.

- Cut 1 H block and 1 D block for Trail 25.

- Cut 1 B block, 1 C block, 1 X block, 1 CR block, and 1 FR block for Trail 35.

- Cut 1 B block and 1 D block for Trail 41.

Lime-green print

- Cut 1 HR block, 7 CR blocks, 1 XR block, 2 C blocks, 1 X block, 1 CR block, and 1 DR block for Trail 24.

- Cut 1 ER block, 1 CR block, 1 XR block, 1 C block, and 1 D block for Trail 29.

- Cut 1 ER block, 3 CR blocks, and 1 FR block for Trail 33.

Assorted fabrics

- Cut 300 J pieces for the circles.

- Cut 16 I pieces for the inserts.

Binding

- Cut 13 strips 2½″ × WOF.

Elements of the Design

TRAILS

Trail 1

1. Lay out the fabric pieces for 12 C blocks to form a circle.

2. Referring to Block Construction, Counterclockwise Blocks (page 15), complete Trail 1.

Trail 1

Trail 2 and Trail 11

1. Lay out the fabric pieces for 1 E block and 1 F block in order.

2. Referring to Block Construction, Counterclockwise Blocks (page 15) complete Trail 2.

3. Make 2 for Trails 2 and 11.

Trail 2

Trail 5

1. Lay out the fabric pieces for 1 H block and 1 F block in order.

2. Referring to Block Construction, Counterclockwise Blocks (page 15) complete Trail 5.

Trail 5

Trail 6 and Trail 41

1. Layout the fabric pieces for 1 B block and 1 D block in order.

2. Referring to Block Construction, Counterclockwise Blocks (page 15) complete Trail 6.

3. Make 2 for Trails 6 and 41.

Trail 6

Trail 12

1. Lay out the fabric pieces for 1 BR block and 1 DR block in order.

2. Referring to Block Construction (page 14) complete Trail 12.

Trail 12

Trail 23 and Trail 25

1. Lay out the fabric pieces for 1 H block and 1 D block in order.

2. Referring to Block Construction, Counterclockwise Blocks (page 15) complete Trail 22.

3. Make 2 for Trails 23 and 25.

Trail 23

Trail 32 and Trail 37

1. Lay out the fabric pieces for 1 ER block and 1 FR block in order.

2. Referring to Block Construction (page 14) complete Trail 32.

3. Make 2 for Trails 32 and 37.

Trail 32

Trail 38

1. Layout the fabric pieces for 1 B block and 1 F block in order.

2. Referring to Block Construction, Counterclockwise Blocks (page 15) complete Trail 38.

Trail 38

Trail 40

1. Lay out the fabric pieces for 1 BR block and 1 FR block in order.

2. Referring to Block Construction (page 14) complete Trail 40.

Trail 40

Trail 15

1. Lay out the fabric pieces for 1 E block, 3 C blocks, and 1 D block in order.

2. Referring to Block Construction, Counterclockwise Blocks (page 15) complete Trail 15.

Trail 15

Trail 19

1. Lay out the fabric pieces for 1 BR block, 3 CR blocks, and 1 FR block in order.

2. Referring to Block Construction (page 14) complete Trail 19.

Trail 19

Trail 33 and Trail 36

1. Lay out the fabric pieces for 1 ER block, 3 CR blocks, and 1 FR block in order.

2. Referring to Block Construction (page 14) complete Trail 33.

3. Make 2 for Trails 33 and 36.

Trail 33

Trail 3

1. Lay out the fabric pieces for 1 E block, 6 C blocks, and 1 F block in order.

2. Referring to Block Construction, Counterclockwise Blocks (page 15) complete Trail 3.

Trail 3

Trail 4 and Trail 9

1. Lay out the fabric pieces for 1 HR block, 6 CR blocks, and 1 DR block in order.

2. Referring to Block Construction (page 14) complete Trail 4.

3. Make 2 for Trails 4 and 9.

Trail 4

Trail 7

1. Referring to Block Construction (page 14) complete Trail 7.

2. Lay out the fabric pieces for 1 HR block, 1 CR block, 1 XR block, 1 C block, and 1 F block in order.

Trail 7

3. Sew the arrows to the neighboring unit.

Sew on arrows.

4. Working from the back, sew units of 1 side together first, then the other.

Join units of each side.

5. Sew the 2 halves together to complete Trail 7. *If the spine doesn't match up check the orientation of template K/KR first. An error is easily made with this piece.*

Trail 7

Trail 14

1. Lay out the fabric pieces for 1 ER block, 1 CR block, 1 XR block, 1 C block, and 1 F block in order.

2. Referring to Block Construction (page 14) complete Trail 14.

Trail 14

Trail 26

1. Lay out the fabric pieces for 1HR block, 1 CR block, 1 XR block, 1 C block, and 1 F block in order.

2. Referring to Block Construction (page 14) complete Trail 26.

Trail 26

Trail 27

1. Lay out the fabric pieces for 1 BR block, 1 CR block, 1 XR block, 1 C block, and 1 D block in order.

2. Referring to Block Construction Counterclockwise Blocks (page 15) complete Trail 27.

Trail 27

Trail 29

1. Lay out the fabric pieces for 1 ER block, 1 CR block, 1 XR block, 1 C block, and 1 D block in order.

2. Referring to Block Construction (page 14) complete Trail 29.

Trail 29

Trail 35

1. Lay out the fabric pieces for 1 B block, 1 C block, 1 X block, 1 CR block, and 1 FR block in order.

2. Referring to Block Construction, Counterclockwise Blocks (page 15) complete Trail 35.

Trail 35

Trail 8

1. Lay out the fabric pieces for 1 BR block, 4 CR blocks, 1 XR block, 1 C block, and 1 D block in order.

2. Referring to Block Construction (page 14) complete Trail 8.

Trail 8

Trail 13

1. Lay out the fabric pieces for 1 H block, 1 C block, 1 X block, 4 CR blocks, and 1 FR block in order.

2. Referring to Block Construction, Counterclockwise Blocks (page 15) complete Trail 13.

Trail 13

Trail 16

1. Lay out the fabric pieces for 1 HR block, 4 CR block, 1 XR block, 1 C block, and 1 D block in order.

2. Referring to Block Construction (page 14) complete Trail 16.

3. Make 2 for Trails 16 and 17.

Trail 16

Trail 18

1. Lay out the fabric pieces for 1 HR block, 4 CR blocks, 1 XR block, 1 C block, and 1F block in order.

2. Referring to Block Construction (page 14) complete Trail 18.

Trail 18

Trail 20

1. Lay out the fabric pieces for 1 ER block, 4 CR blocks, 1 XR block, 1 C block, and 1 D block in order.

2. Referring to Block Construction (page 14) complete Trail 16.

Trail 20

Trail 31

1. Lay out the fabric pieces for 1 B block, 4 C blocks, 1 X block, 1 CR block, and 1 FR block in order.

2. Referring to Block Construction, Counterclockwise Blocks (page 15) complete Trail 31.

Trail 31

Trail 39

1. Lay out the fabric pieces for 1 BR block, 4 CR block, 1 XR block, 1 C block, and 1 F block in order.

2. Referring to Block Construction (page 14) complete Trail 39.

Trail 39

Trail 34

1. Lay out the fabric pieces for 1 B block, 4 C blocks, 1 X block, 7 CR blocks, and 1 FR block in order.

2. Referring to Block Construction, Counterclockwise Blocks (page 15) complete Trail 34.

Trail 22

1. Lay out the fabric pieces for 1 ER block, 1 CR block, 1 XR block, 5 C blocks, 1 X block, 1 CR block, and 1 DR block in order.

2. Referring to Block Construction (page 14) complete Trail 22.

Trail 10

1. Lay out the fabric pieces for 1 H block, 1 C block, 1 X block, 2 CR blocks, 1 XR block, 4 C blocks, and 1 F block in order.

2. Referring to Block Construction, Counterclockwise Blocks (page 15) complete Trail 10.

Trail 21

1. Lay out the fabric pieces for 1 HR block, 4 CR blocks, 1 XR block, 2 C blocks, 1 X block, 1 CR block, and 1 FR block in order.

2. Referring to Block Construction (page 14) complete Trail 21.

Trail 34

Trail 22

Trail 10

Trail 21

Trail 24

1. Lay out the fabric pieces for 1 HR block, 7 CR blocks, 1 XR block, 2 C blocks, 1 X block, 1 CR block, and 1 DR block in order.

2. Referring to Block Construction (page 14) complete Trail 24.

Trail 28

1. Lay out the fabric pieces for 1 HR block, 7 CR blocks, 1 XR block, 2 C blocks, 1 X block, 1 CR block, and 1 FR block in order.

2. Referring to Block Construction (page 14) complete Trail 28.

Trail 30

1. Lay out the fabric pieces for 1 HR block, 1 CR block, 1 XR block, 5 C blocks, 1 X block, 1 CR block, and 1 FR block in order.

2. Referring to Block Construction (page 14) complete Trail 30.

Trail 24

Trail 28

Trail 30

CIRCLES

Referring to Making the Circles (page 10) make 25 circles. Check that they are sized correctly and redraw the outer sewing/cutting line if necessary. Referring to the quilt layout diagram (page 61) place them in the quilt and label them.

JOINING TRAILS, INSERTS, AND CIRCLES

Refer to Joining Paths and Circles (page 15) and Joining Crossover Blocks to Circle (page 15).

Some seams are initially basted as there is only 1 definite matching point. *Place 2 safety pins in basted seams to make it easy to find them again later.*

Later when joining to places that have only been basted sew the original seams securely.

Inserts

Sew an insert to Trails 2, 5, 6, 11, 12, 23, 25, 32, 37, 38, 40 and 41.

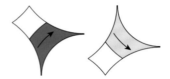

Trail and insert

Unit A

Sew circle A, 9 J pieces to Trail 34, 7 CR, and FR blocks. Label this Unit A.

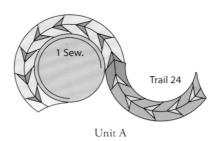

Unit A

Unit B

1. Match circle B, 5 J pieces to Trail 31, 4 C blocks, and up to the matching point of the X block.

2. Baste circle B to Trail 31, B block.

3. Sew circle B, 5 J pieces to Trail 31, 4 C blocks, and up to the matching point of the X block.

4. Baste circle B to Trail 31, the remainder of the X block. Label this Unit B.

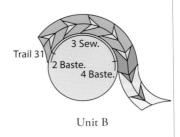

Unit B

Unit C

1. Sew circle C, 6 J pieces to Trail 33, FR, 3 CR, and ER blocks.

2. Sew circle C, 3 J pieces to Trail 32, FR, and ER blocks. Label this Unit C.

Unit C

Unit D and Unit X

1. Match circle D, 7 J pieces to Trail 9, 6 CR blocks, and up to the matching point of the DR block.

2. Baste circle D to Trail 9, HR block.

3. Sew circle D, 7 J pieces to Trail 9, 6 CR blocks, and up to the matching point of the DR block.

4. Baste circle D to Trail 9, the remainder of the DR block. Label this Unit D.

5. Repeat with circle X and Trail 4. Label this Unit X.

Unit D

Unit E

1. Match circle E, 8 J pieces to Trail 24, 7 CR blocks, and up to the matching point of the XR block.

2. Baste circle E to Trail 24, HR block.

3. Sew circle E, 8 J pieces to Trail 24, 7 CR blocks, and up to the matching point of the XR block.

4. Baste circle E to Trail 24, the remainder of the XR block. Label this Unit E.

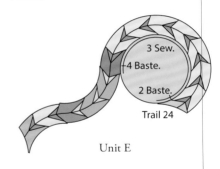

Unit E

Unit F

1. Sew circle F, 2 J pieces to Trail 38, F block.

2. Baste circle F to Trail 38, B block. Label this Unit F.

Unit F

Unit G

1. Sew circle G, 6 J pieces to Trail 36, ER, 3 CR, and FR blocks.

2. Sew circle G, 3 J pieces to Trail 37, ER, and FR blocks. Label this Unit G.

Unit G

Unit H

Matching a seam in circle H to Trail 25, the seam between H and D blocks, baste circle H to Trail 25, H and D blocks. Label this Unit H.

Unit H

Unit I

1. Match circle I, 2 J pieces to Trail 10, 1 C, and up to the matching point of the X block.

2. Baste circle I to Trail 10, H block.

3. Sew circle I, 2 J pieces to Trail 10, 1 C, and up to the matching point of the X block.

4. Baste circle I to Trail 10, the remainder of the X block.

5. Sew circle O, 6 J pieces to Trail 10, 4 C, and F blocks.

6. Sew circle O, 3 J pieces to Trail 11, E, and F blocks. Label this Unit I.

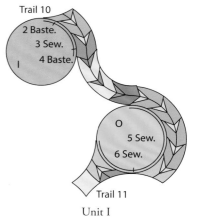

Unit I

Unit J

Matching a seam in circle J to Trail 23, seam between the H and D blocks, baste circle J to Trail 23, H, and D blocks. Label this Unit J.

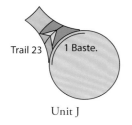

Unit J

Unit K

1. Match circle K, 5 J pieces to Trail 39, 4 CR blocks, and up to the matching point of the XR block.

2. Baste circle K to Trail 39, BR block.

3. Sew circle K, 5 J pieces to Trail 39, 4 C blocks, and up to the matching point of the X block.

4. Baste circle K to Trail 39, the remainder of the X block. Label this Unit K.

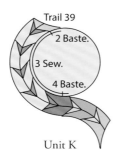

Unit K

Unit L

1. Match circle L, 5 J pieces to Trail 16, 4 CR blocks, and up to the matching point of the XR block.

2. Baste circle L to Trail 16, HR block.

3. Sew circle L, 5 J pieces to Trail 16, 4 CR blocks, and up to the matching point of the XR block.

4. Baste circle L to Trail 16, the remainder of XR block. Label this Unit L.

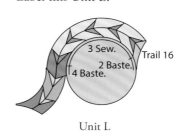

Unit L

Unit M

1. Match circle M, 5 J pieces to Trail 15, E, 3 C blocks, and up to the matching point of the D block.

2. Baste circle M to Trail 15, B block.

3. Sew circle M, 5 J pieces to Trail 15, E, 3 C blocks, and up to the matching point of the D block.

4. Baste circle M to Trail 15, the remainder of D block. Label this Unit M.

Unit M

Unit N

1. Sew circle N, 6 J pieces to Trail 22, 5 C blocks, and up to the matching point of the X block.

2. Baste circle N to Trail 22, the remainder of the X block. Label this Unit N.

Unit N

Unit P

1. Match circle P, 5 J pieces to Trail 17, 4 CR blocks, and up to the matching point of the XR block.

2. Baste circle P to Trail 17, HR block.

3. Sew circle P, 5 J pieces to Trail 17, 4 CR blocks, and up to the matching point of the XR block.

4. Baste circle P to Trail 17, the remainder of the XR block. Label this Unit P.

Unit P

Unit Q

1. Sew circle Q, 2 J pieces to Trail 40, FR block.

2. Baste circle Q to Trail 40, BR block. Label this Unit Q.

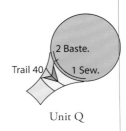

Unit Q

Unit R

1. Baste circle R to Trail 19, BR block, matching the seam between BR block and CR block to a seam from the circle.

2. Sew circle R, 5 J pieces to Trail 19, 4 CR and FR blocks. Label this Unit R.

Unit R

Unit S

1. Match circle S, 2 J pieces to Trail 5, F block.

2. Baste circle S to Trail 5, H block.

3. Sew circle S, 2 J pieces to Trail 5, F block.

4. Baste circle S to Trail 6, B, and D blocks. Label this Unit S.

Unit S

Unit T

Sew circle T, 12 J pieces to Trail 1, 12 C blocks. Label this Unit T.

An error was made when cutting fabric for the original quilt. The instructions have been changed to eliminate the error and all of the arrows now go in 1 direction.

Unit T

Unit U

1. Match circle U, 8 J pieces to Trail 28, 7 CR blocks, and up to the matching point of the XR block.

2. Baste circle U to Trail 28, HR block.

3. Sew circle U, 8 J pieces to Trail 28, 7 CR blocks, and up to the matching point of the XR block.

4. Baste circle U to Trail 28, the remainder of the XR block. Label this Unit U.

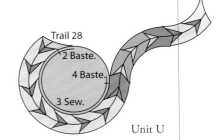

Unit U

Unit V

1. Match circle V, 5 J pieces to Trail 18, 4 CR blocks, and up to the matching point of the XR block.

2. Baste circle V to Trail 18, HR block.

3. Sew circle V, 5 J pieces to Trail 18, 4 CR blocks, and up to the matching point of the XR block.

4. Baste circle V to Trail 18, the remainder of the XR block. Label this Unit V.

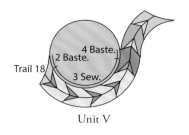

Unit V

Unit W

1. Match circle W, 5 J pieces to Trail 21, 4 CR blocks, and up to the matching point of the XR block.

2. Baste circle W to Trail 21, HR block.

3. Sew circle W, 5 J pieces to Trail 21, 4 CR blocks, and up to the matching point of the XR block.

4. Baste circle W to Trail 21, the remainder of the XR block. Label this Unit W.

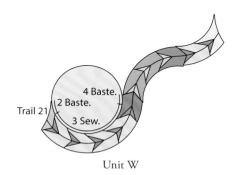

Unit W

Unit Y

1. Sew circle Y, 3 J pieces to Trail 2, E, and F blocks.

2. Sew circle Y, 9 J pieces to Trail 3, E, 6C, and F blocks.

3. Label this Unit Y.

Unit Y

JOINING THE TRAILS

On a flat surface lay out the Trails as directed. Where there are no matching points, pin the ends then find midpoints and quarter points. Match these and sew them together. When joining to places that have only been basted check that the fabrics are lying flat, without stretching or puckering, and sew the original seams securely.

Some seams will again only be basted initially. *Place 2 safety pins in basted seams to make it easy to find them again later* and sew securely at that stage.

Unit LA

Unit F and Trail 35

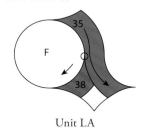

Unit LA

1. Match Trail 35, X block overhang to Trail 38, B block short side.

2. Match Trail 35, FR block corner to the insert corner.

3. Match the quarter points of the insert and Trail 38 back to Trail 35, FR, and CR blocks. Sew.

4. Sew Trail 38, basted B block and Trail 35, X and C blocks to circle F, 3 J pieces.

5. Baste Trail 35 to circle F.

6. Label this Unit LA.

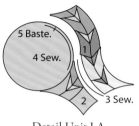

Detail Unit LA

Unit LB

Unit J and Trail 8

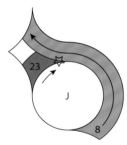

Unit LB

1. Match Trail 8, XR block overhang to Trail 23, D block short side.

2. Match Trail 8, D block corner to the insert corner.

3. Match the quarter points of the insert and Trail 23 front to Trail 8, D, and C blocks. Sew.

4. Match the quarter points of Trail 23, basted D block, and Trail 8, XR, and 4 CR blocks to circle J, 7 J pieces. Sew.

5. Baste Trail 8, BR block to circle J.

6. Label this Unit LB.

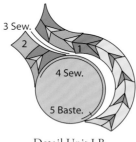

Detail Unit LB

Unit LC

Unit H, Trails 13 and 14

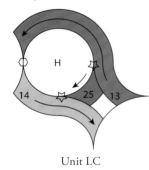

Unit LC

1. Match Trail 25, H block short side to Trail 13, CR block overhang.

2. Match Trail 13, H block corner to the insert corner.

3. Match the quarter points of the insert and Trail 25 back to Trail 13, H, C, and X blocks. Sew.

4. Sew Trail 13, 4 CR and FR blocks to circle H, 6 J pieces.

5. Match Trail 14, XR block overhang to Trail 25, D block short side.

6. Match the quarter points of Trail 14, ER, CR, XR, and basted Trail 25 to circle H, 6 J pieces. Sew.

7. Match Trail 14, F block corner to the insert corner.

8. Match the quarter points of Trail 14, C, and F block to Trail 25 front and the insert. Sew.

9. Label this Unit LC.

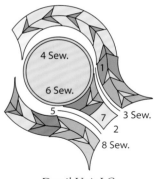

Detail Unit LC

Unit LD

Unit Q and Trail 27

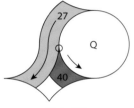

Unit LD

1. Match Trail 27, XR block overhang to Trail 40, BR block short side.

2. Sew Trail 40, BR block and Trail 27, XR and CR blocks to circle Q, 3 J pieces.

3. Baste Trail 27, BR block to circle Q.

4. Match Trail 27, D block corner to the insert corner.

5. Match the quarter points of the Trail 27, C, and D blocks to Trail 40 back and the insert. Sew.

6. Label this Unit LD.

Detail Unit LD

Unit LE

Unit R and Trail 20

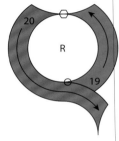

Unit LE

1. Match Trail 20, XR block overhang to Trail 19, BR block short side.

2. Match the quarter points of Trail 20, ER, 4 CR, XR blocks, and Trail 19, basted BR block to circle R, 7 J segments. Sew.

3. Sew Trail 19 back to Trail 20 outer edge.

4. Label this Unit LE.

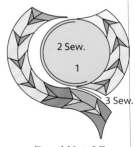

Detail Unit LE

Unit LF

Unit V and Trail 18

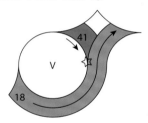

Unit L

1. Match Trail 18, XR block overhang to Trail 41, D block short side.

2. Match Trail 18, F block corner to the insert corner.

3. Match the quarter points of Trail 18, F, and C blocks to the insert and Trail 41 front. Sew.

4. Match the quarter points of Trail 18, basted XR block and Trail 41, D block to circle V, 3 J segments. Baste.

5. Label this Unit LF.

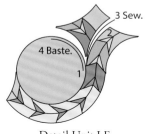

Detail Unit LF

Unit LG

Units A, B and C

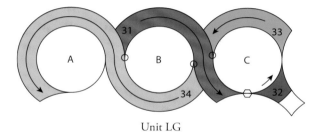

Unit LG

1. Match Trail 31, X block overhang to Trail 34, B block short side.

2. Match Trail 34, X block overhang to Trail 31, B block short side.

3. Sew Trail 31, basted X block, Trail 34, B, 4 C, X blocks, and Trail 31, basted B block to circle B, 7 J segments.

4. Sew Trail 31 back to Trail 34 outer edge.

5. Match Trail 31, CR block overhang to Trail 33, FR short side.

6. Sew Trail 31, FR and CR blocks to circle C, 3 J pieces.

7. Sew Trail 33 front to Trail 31 outer edge.

8. Label this Unit LG.

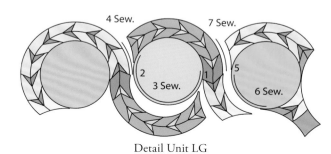

Detail Unit LG

Unit LH

Unit LA and Trail 30

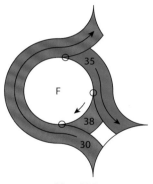

Unit LH

1. Match Trail 30, X block overhang to Trail 35, B block short side.

2. Match Trail 30, C block overhang Trail 38, F block short side.

3. Match Trail 30, HR block corner to the insert corner.

4. Match the quarter points of Trail 30, HR, CR, and XR blocks to the insert and Trail 38 front. Sew.

5. Sew Trail 30, 5 C and X blocks and Trail 35, basted B block to circle F, 7 J segments.

6. Sew Trail 35 back to Trail 30 outer edge.

7. Label this Unit LH.

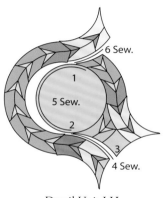

Detail Unit LH

Unit LI

Units E and LB

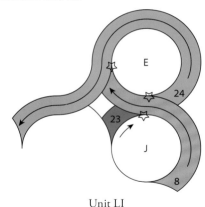

Unit LI

1. Match Trail 24, XR block overhang to Trail 8, D block short side.

2. Match Trail 8, CR block overhang to Trail 24, DR block short side.

3. Match the quarter points of Trail 24, basted XR block, Trail 8, D and C blocks, and Trail 24, basted HR block to circle E, 4 J segments. Sew.

4. Sew Trail 24 back to Trail 8 outer edge.

5. Baste Trail 8 front and the insert to Trail 24 outer edge.

6. Label this Unit LI.

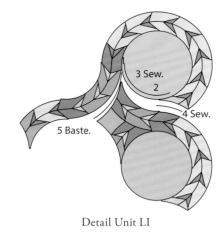

Detail Unit LI

Unit LJ

Units N and I, Trails 7 and 12

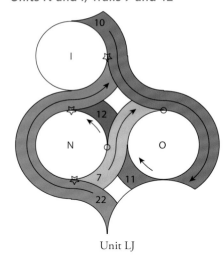

Unit LJ

1. Match Trail 22, X block overhang to Trail 12, DR block short side.

2. Match Trail 7, XR block overhang to Trail 12, BR block short side.

3. Match Trail 22, C block overhang to Trail 7, HR block short side.

4. Match the quarter points of Trail 7, HR, CR, and XR blocks, Trail 12, BR and DR blocks, and Trail 22, basted X block to circle N, 6 J pieces. Sew.

5. Match the quarter points of the insert and Trail 12 front to Trail 22, DR, and CR blocks. Sew

6. Match the quarter points of the insert and Trail 12 back to Trail 7, F, and C blocks. Sew.

7. Sew Trail 7 back to Trail 22 outer edge.

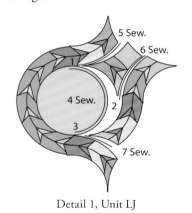

Detail 1, Unit LJ

8. Match Trail 10, X block overhang to Trail 22, DR block short side.

9. Match Trail 10, C block overhang to Trail 7, F block short side.

10. Match the quarter points of Trail 10, 2 CR, and XR blocks to Trail 22 front, the insert, and Trail 7 front. Sew.

11. Match Trail 7, C block overhang to Trail 11, F block short side.

12. Match the quarter points of Trail 7, HR, CR, and XR blocks to the insert and Trail 11 front. Sew.

13. Sew Trail 7, C, and F blocks to circle O, 3 J segments.

14. Match the quarter points of Trail 7 back and the insert to Trail 22, XR, CR, and ER blocks. Sew.

15. Match the quarter points of Trail 10, basted X block, and Trail 22, DR, and CR blocks to circle I, 3 J segments. Sew.

16. Label this Unit LJ.

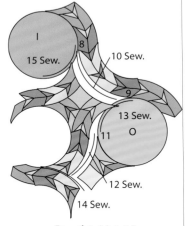

Detail 2, Unit LJ

Unit LK

Units D and LI

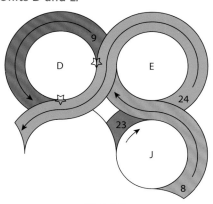

Unit LK

1. Match Trail 24, X block overhang to Trail 9, DR block short side.

2. Sew Trail 9 front to Trail 24 outer edge.

3. Match Trail 24, C block overhang to Trail 9, HR block short side.

4. Sew Trail 9 back to Trail 24 outer edge.

5. Match the quarter points of Trail 9, basted HR block, Trail 24, 2 C and X blocks, and Trail 9, basted DR block to circle D, 6 J pieces. Sew.

6. Label this Unit LK.

Detail Unit LK

Unit LL

Units LJ and LK

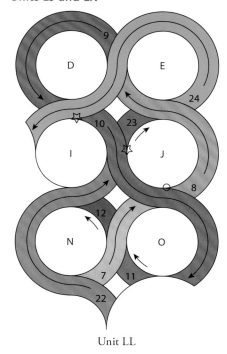

Unit LL

1. Match Trail 10, CR block overhang to Trail 23, H block short side.

2. Match the quarter points of the insert and Trail 23 back to Trail 10, H, C, and X blocks. Sew.

3. Match Trail 10, XR block overhang to Trail 8, BR block short side.

4. Sew Trail 8 back to Trail 10 outer edge.

5. Match the quarter points of Trail 23, basted H block, Trail 10, 2 CR, and XR blocks, and Trail 8, basted BR block to circle J. Sew.

6. Match Trail 24, CR block overhang to Trail 10, H block short side.

7. Match the quarter points of basted Trail 8 front, the insert, and Trail 10 back to Trail 24, 2 C, and X blocks. Adjust if necessary. Sew.

8. Baste Trail 24, CR, and DR blocks to circle I.

9. Label this Unit LL.

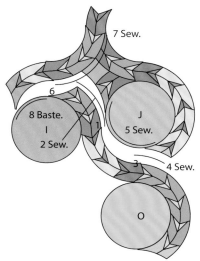

Detail Unit LL

Unit LM

Units K and L, Trails 26 and 29

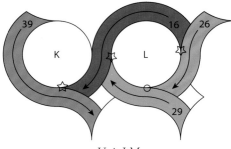

Unit LM

1. Baste the insert to the Trail 29 outer edge.

2. Match Trail 16, XR block overhang to Trail 29, D block short side.

3. Match the quarter points of the insert and Trail 29 front to Trail 16, D, and C blocks. Sew.

4. Baste the insert to the Trail 26 outer edge.

5. Match Trail 29, C block overhang to Trail 26, F block short side.

6. Match the quarter points of the insert and Trail 26 front to Trail 29, ER, CR, and XR blocks. Sew.

7. Match Trail 26, C block overhang to Trail 16, HR block short side.

8. Sew Trail 16 back to Trail 26 outer edge.

9. Match the quarter points of Trail 16, basted XR block, Trail 29, D and C blocks, Trail 26, F and C blocks, and Trail 16 HR block to circle L, 7 J pieces. Sew.

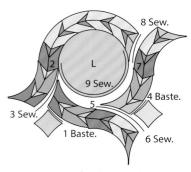

Detail 1, Unit LM

10. Match Trail 39, XR block overhang to Trail 16, D block short side.

11. Match the quarter points of the insert and Trail 16 front to Trail 39, F, and C blocks. Sew.

12. Match the quarter points of Trail 16, C and D blocks, and Trail 39, basted XR block to circle K, 3 J pieces. Sew.

13. Label this Unit LM.

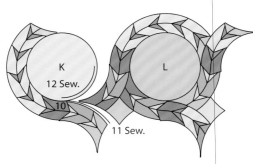

Detail 2, Unit LM

Unit LN

Units P, U, and LD

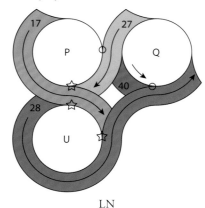

LN

1. Match Trail 17, XR block overhang to Trail 27, D block short side.

2. Match the quarter points of Trail 27 front and the insert to Trail 17, C, and D blocks. Sew.

3. Baste Trail 27, C and D blocks to circle P.

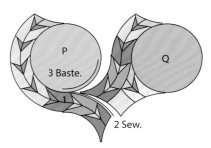

Detail 1, Unit LN

4. Match Trail 28, CR overhang to Trail 40, FR block short side.

5. Match Trail 28, XR overhang to Trail 17, D block short side.

6. Sew Trail 28, FR and CR blocks to circle Q, 3 J segments.

7. Match the quarter points of Trail 40 front, the insert, and Trail 17 front to Trail 28, X, and 2 C blocks. Sew.

8. Match Trail 17, C block overhang to Trail 28, HR block short side.

9. Match the quarter points of Trail 28, basted HR block, Trail 17, C and D blocks, and Trail 28, basted XR block to circle U. Sew.

10. Sew Trail 28 back to Trail 17 outer edge.

11. Label this Unit LN.

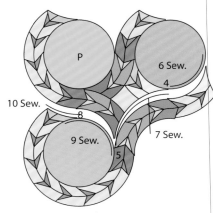

Detail 2, Unit LN

Unit LO

Units LM and LN

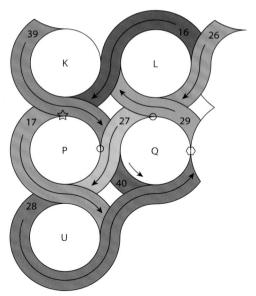

Unit LO

5. Match Trail 27, C block overhang to Trail 39, F block short side.

6. Match the quarter points of the insert and Trail 39 front to Trail 27, BR, CR, and XR blocks. Sew.

7. Match Trail 39, C block overhang to Trail 17, HR block short side.

8. Match the quarter points of Trail 17, basted XR block, Trail 27, D and C blocks, Trail 39, F and C blocks, and Trail 17, HR block to circle P, 7 J segments. Sew.

9. Sew Trail 17 back to Trail 39 outer edge.

10. Label this Unit LO.

1. Match Trail 29, ER block short side to Trail 28, FR block short side.

2. Match Trail 29, XR block overhang to Trail 27, BR block short side.

3. Match the quarter points of basted the insert and Trail 27 back to Trail 29, D and C blocks. Sew.

4. Match the quarter points of Trail 27, basted BR block, and Trail 29, XR, CR, and ER blocks to circle Q. Sew.

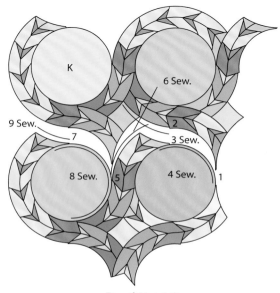

Detail Unit LO

Unit LP

Units S and LE

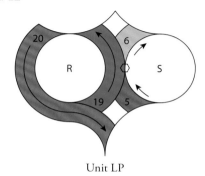

Unit LP

1. Match the quarter points of the insert, Trail 6 back, Trail 5 front, and the insert to Trail 19, FR, 3 CR, and BR blocks. Sew.

2. Match the quarter points of the insert and Trail 19 back to Trail 20, D and C blocks. Sew.

3. Label this Unit LP.

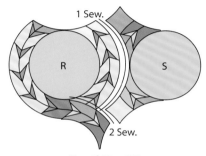

Detail Unit LP

Unit LQ

Units W and LF

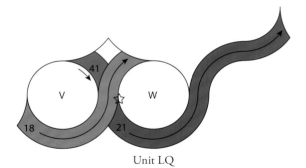

Unit LQ

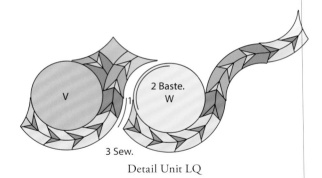

Detail Unit LQ

1. Match Trail 18, C block overhang to Trail 21, HR block short side.

2. Baste Trail 18, F and C blocks to circle W.

3. Sew Trail 21 back to Trail 18 outer edge.

4. Label this Unit LQ.

Unit LR

Units M, LP and LQ

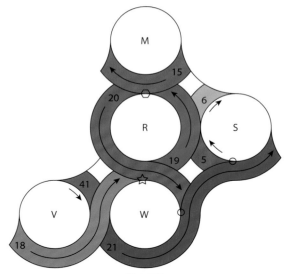

Unit LR

1. Match Trail 21, CR block overhang to Trail 5, H block short side.

2. Match Trail 21, XR block overhang to Trail 20, D block short side.

3. Baste Trail 21, FR and CR blocks and Trail 5, H block to circle S.

4. Match the quarter points of Trail 21, X and 2C blocks to Trail 5 back, the insert, and Trail 20 front. Sew.

5. Match Trail 20, block C overhang to Trail 18, F block short side.

6. Match the quarter points of Trail 21, basted XR block, Trail 20, D and C blocks, Trail 18, F and C blocks and Trail 21, HR block to circle W, 7 J segments. Sew.

7. Baste Trail 18 front and the insert to Trail 20 outer edge.

8. Match the insert corner to Trail 15 back corner.

9. Baste the insert, Trail 19 front and Trail 20 back to Trail 15 outer edge.

10. Label this Unit LR.

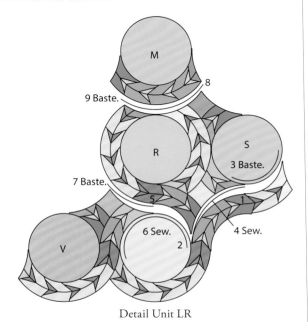

Detail Unit LR

Unit LS

Units G, LC and LH

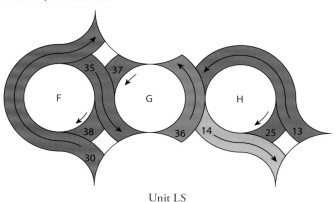

Unit LS

1. Match Trail 35, FR block short side to Trail 36, ER block short side.

2. Match Trail 37, FR block short side to Trail 35, CR block overhang.

3. Match Trail 35 back corner to the insert corner.

4. Match the quarter points of Trail 35, FR, CR, X, C, and B blocks to circle G, 3 J pieces, Trail 37 front, and the insert.

5. Match Trail 30 front corner to the insert corner.

6. Sew the basted Trail 35 back and the insert to Trail 30, CR, and FR blocks.

7. Pin-mark the center of Trail 36. Match this to the middle between Trail 13 front and Trail 14 back.

8. Baste Trail 14 back and Trail 13 front to Trail 36 outer edge.

9. Label this unit LS.

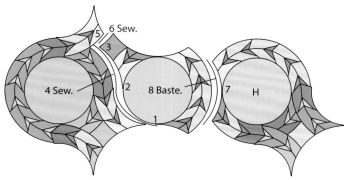

Detail Unit LS

Unit LT

Units T, X and Y

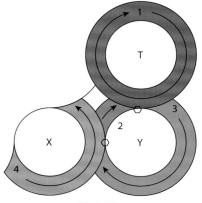

Unit LT

1. Baste the insert, Trail 2 front and Trail 3 back to Trail 1 outer edge.

2. Baste the insert, Trail 2 back, and Trail 3 front to Trail 4 outer edge.

3. Label this Unit LT.

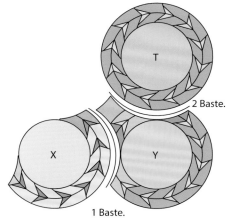

Detail Unit LT

Unit LU

Units LG and LS

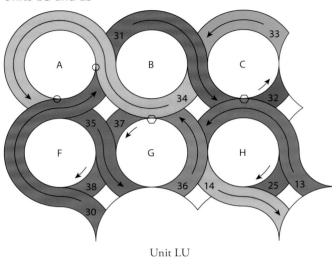

Unit LU

1. Match Trail 34, CR block overhang to Trail 30, FR block short side.

2. Match Trail 30, CR block overhang to Trail 34, FR block short side.

3. Sew Trail 30, F, and C blocks to circle A, 3J pieces.

4. Sew Trail 34 front to Trail 30 outer edge.

5. Match the insert corner to Trail 31 front corner.

6. Match the midpoints of the insert and Trail 34 back to Trail 31, CR, and FR blocks. Sew.

7. Match the insert corner to Trail 13 front corner.

8. Match the midpoints of the insert and Trail 13 front to Trail 36 outer edge. Sew.

9. Match the quarter points of Trail 30 front, the insert, Trail 37 back, Trail 36 front, and the insert to Trail 34, B, 4C, and X blocks. Sew.

10. Baste the insert, Trail 31 front, Trail 32 back, and the insert to Trail 13 outer edge.

11. Match the midpoints of the insert and basted Trail 14 back to Trail 36 outer edge. Sew.

12. Baste the insert to Trail 14 outer edge.

13. Label this Unit LU.

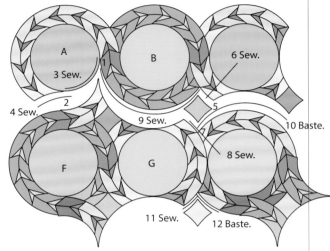

Detail Unit LU

Unit LV

Units LO and LR

1. Match Trail 26, XR block overhang to Trail 15, D block short side.

2. Baste Trail 26, HR, CR, and XR blocks to circle M.

3. Match the midpoints of Trail 15 front and basted insert to Trail 26, C, and F blocks. Sew.

4. Match Trail 28 front corner to the insert corner.

5. Match the quarter points of the insert, Trail 29 back, Trail 28 front, basted insert, and Trail 18 front to Trail 20, ER, 4 CR, and XR blocks. Sew.

6. Match Trail 28, X block overhang to Trail 41, B block short side.

7. Match the midpoints of Trail 28, FR, and CR blocks to the insert and Trail 41 back. Sew.

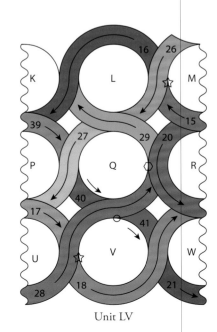

Unit LV

8. Match Trail 28, C block overhang to Trail 18, HR block short side.

9. Match the quarter points of Trail 18, basted XR block, Trail 41, D and B blocks, Trail 28, X and 2 C blocks, and Trail 18, HR block to circle V, 7 J segments. Sew.

10. Sew Trail 18 back to Trail 28 outer edge.

11. Label this Unit LV.

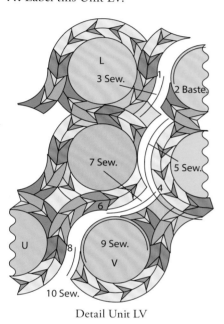

Detail Unit LV

Unit LW

Units LU and LV

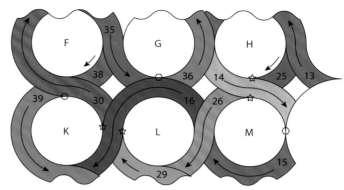

Unit LW section

1. Match Trail 14, C block overhang to Trail 26, HR block short side.

2. Match Trail 14, F block short side to Trail 15, E block short side.

3. Match the quarter points of Trail 15, basted B block, Trail 14, F and C blocks, and Trail 26, basted HR block to circle M. Sew.

4. Match Trail 26, HR back corner to the insert corner.

5. Match the quarter points of Trail 14, XR, CR, and ER blocks to Trail 26 back and the insert. Sew.

6. Match Trail 16 back corner to the insert corner.

7. Match the quarter points of the insert and Trail 16 back to Trail 26, HR, CR, and XR blocks. Sew.

8. Match Trail 16, C block overhang to Trail 30, HR block short side.

9. Match the quarter points of the insert, Trail 36 back, Trail 35 front, the insert, and Trail 30 back to Trail 16, HR, 4 CR, and XR blocks. Sew.

10. Match Trail 30, XR block overhang to Trail 39, BR block short side.

11. Match the quarter points of Trail 30, HR, CR, and XR blocks and Trail 39, basted BR block to circle K. Sew.

12. Sew Trail 39 back to Trail 30 outer edge.

13. Label this Unit LW.

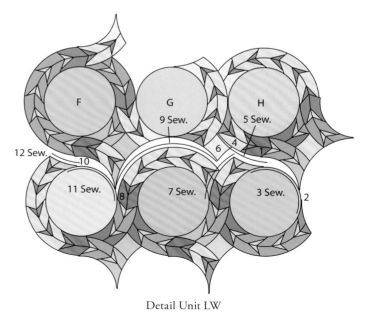

Detail Unit LW

Unit LX

Units LL and LW

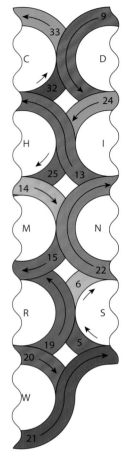

Unit LX section

1. Baste Trail 33 back, Trail 32 front, and the insert to Trail 9 outer edge.

2. Sew the insert and Trail 9 front to Trail 24 outer edge.

3. Match Trail 13, X block overhang to Trail 24, DR block short side.

4. Check and complete basted Trail 13, 4 CR and FR blocks to Trail 24 front, the insert and Trail 32 back, Trail 13 front, and the insert. Sew.

5. Match Trail 22, CR block overhang to Trail 13, H block short side.

6. Match the quarter points of Trail 13, H, C, and X blocks and Trail 24, DR, and CR blocks to circle I, 6 J segments. Sew.

7. Match Trail 22, XR block overhang to Trail 6, D block short side.

8. Match the quarter points of Trail 6 front, the insert, Trail 15 back, Trail 14 front, the insert, Trail 13 back to Trail 22, 5 C, and X blocks. Sew.

9. Match Trail 22, ER block short side to Trail 21, FR block short side.

10. Match the quarter points of Trail 22, ER, CR, and XR blocks and Trail 6, D, and B blocks to circle S, 6 J segments. Sew.

11. Label this Unit LX.

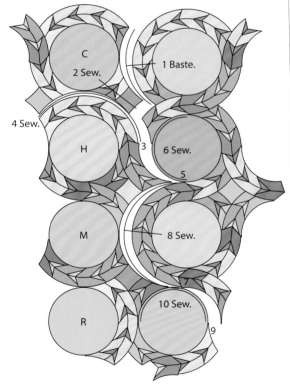

Detail Unit LX

Unit LY = Quilt Center

Units LX and LT

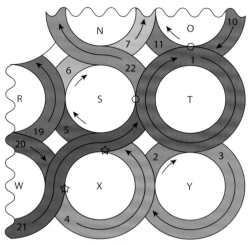

Unit LY section

1. Match Trail 21, X block overhang to Trail 4, DR block short side.

2. Match Trail 21, C block overhang to Trail 4, HR block short side.

3. Match the quarter points of Trail 4, HR block, Trail 21, 2 C and X blocks, and Trail 4, DR block to circle X, 6 J segments. Sew.

4. Sew Trail 4 back to Trail 21 outer edge.

5. Match the midpoints of Trail 4 front and the insert to Trail 21, CR, and FR blocks. Sew.

6. Baste Trail 1 to Trail 10 front, Trail 11 back, the insert, Trail 22 back, Trail 21 front, the insert, Trail 2 front, and Trail 3 back.

7. Check that Trail 1 is placed correctly with no puckers or stretched sections. Sew.

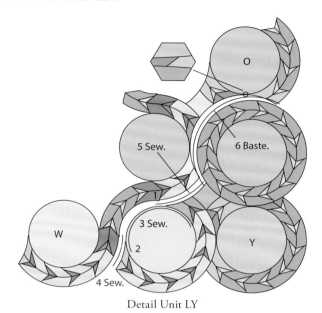

Detail Unit LY

8. Lay your quilt top on a flat surface and check for any safety-pin markers indicating basted seams. Sew these seams securely.

Border

PATTERNS

Refer to Preparing the Background Border Patterns (page 16).

1. Cut a rectangle of freezer paper 10″ × 120″.

2. Draw a line with a ruler 4½″ from a long edge.

3. Draw a 5-circle border following directions (page 17).

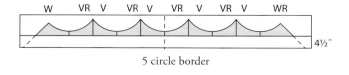

5 circle border

CUTTING

WOF = width of fabric.

Starch and press all fabric before cutting to minimize stretching.

Always mark the center spine with an arrow; it is marked with a double-ended arrow on the template. Refer to The Blocks (page 13) for more information.

Purple Batik

Refer to Marking the Background Border (page 17).

1. Press the 5 circle border freezer-paper template to the wrong side of the fabric rectangle. Trace around the template. The dashed line is the sewing line. The solid line is the cutting line.

2. Leaving at least ½″ between the sewing lines trace around the border freezer-paper template 3 more times.

3. Cut ¼″ from the sewing line of the borders when ready to sew.

ATTACHING THE BORDER

Refer to Attaching the Background Border (page 18). See Trimming the Corners (page 84) after the quilting is completed.

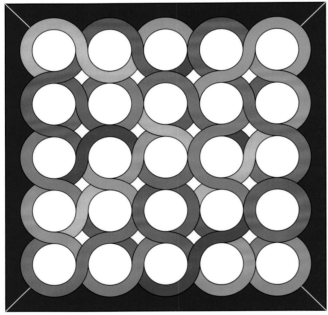

Borders

Finishing the Quilt

1. Cut the backing fabric into 3 equal lengths.

2. Refer to Finishing (page 19).

Quilting

This quilt was hand quilted and ditched stitched with a matching colored thread along every seam after which echo quilting was added. Along the paths, there are 5 parallel rows of quilting, 1 on each edge, 1 in the middle, and a row between the middle and each edge. Circle wedges had 3 extra arcs of quilting and the border was cross-hatched following the curve of the quilt top edge.

Trimming the Corners

After completing the quilting trim away the excess batting and backing. To trim the corners, measure 10″ in from each corner in both directions. Draw a line directly across between these points and stitch a line of basting ⅛″ in from this line. Trim along the marked line.

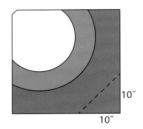

Trim corners.

Binding the Quilt

Using the 2½″ strips, refer to Binding (page 19).

Alternate Path Color Option

MATERIALS

Multicolored Version

Fabrics 1–2: ⅔ yard each for Trails 24 and 34

Fabrics 3–8: ½ yard each for Trails 1, 10, 21, 22, 28, and 30

Fabrics 9–26: ⅓ yard each for Trails 3, 4, 7, 8, 9, 13, 14, 16, 17, 18, 19, 20, 26, 31, 33, 35, 36, and 39

Fabrics 27–41: 1 fat sixteenth each for Trails 2, 5, 6, 11, 12, 15, 23, 25, 27, 29, 32, 37, 38, 40, and 41

 Note

Arrows may be cut from path and wedge fabrics.

Further Designs

All of the quilts presented in this book may be easily combined with circular and hexagonal designs. The selection below combines the layouts in this book with blocks taken from my earlier books, *The Storyteller's Sampler Quilt* and *Dazzling New York Beauty Sampler*. There are many more blocks in both of these books that can be used. Be Creative!

Laneways (page 25) and Reflections block from *The Storyteller's Sampler Quilt*. (Reflections block enlarged 433%)

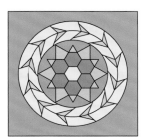

Trail 1 (page 64) and Strawberry Shortcake block from *The Storyteller's Sampler Quilt*. (Strawberry Shortcake block enlarged 433%)

Alleyway (page 20) and Green Tree Frog block from *Dazzling New York Beauty Sampler*.

Tracks (page 50) and blocks from *Dazzling New York Beauty Sampler*.

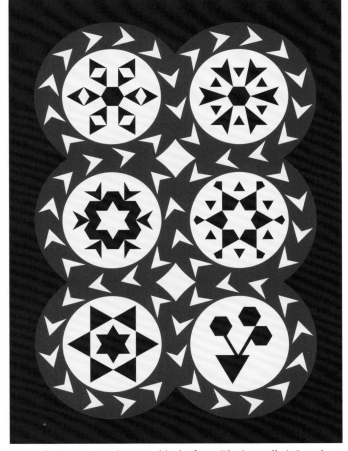

Tracks (page 50) and various blocks from *The Storyteller's Sampler Quilt* (blocks enlarged 433%)

Template Patterns

Template K
Block A

Template I
Insert

Template L
Block A

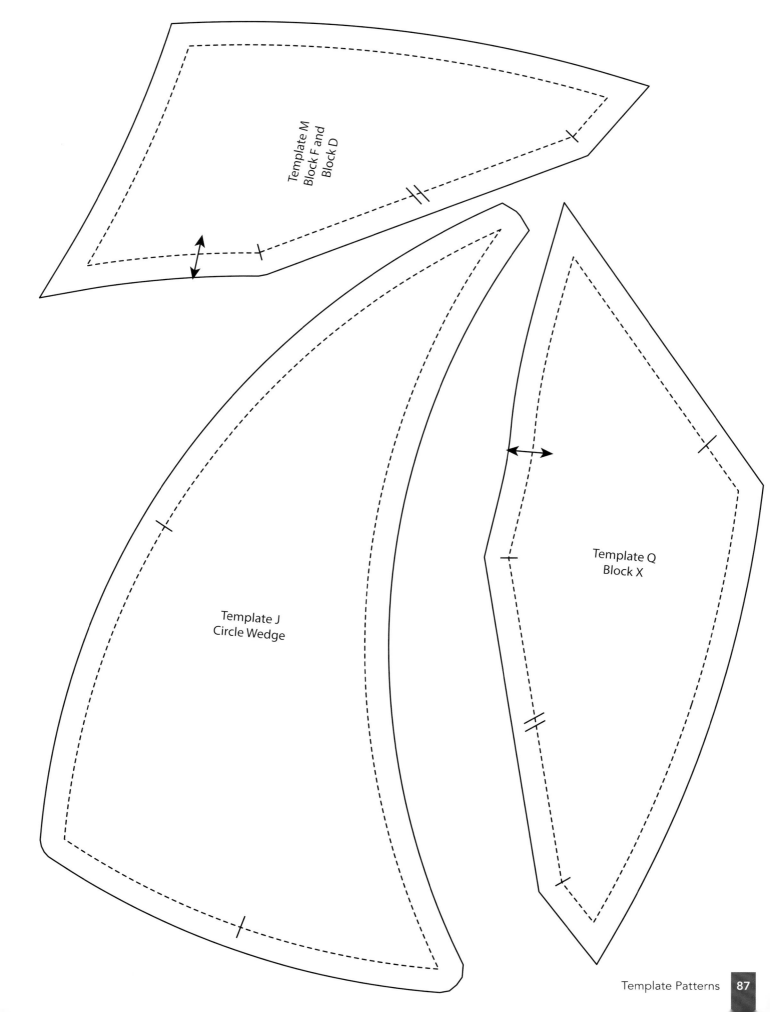

Template M
Block F and
Block D

Template J
Circle Wedge

Template Q
Block X

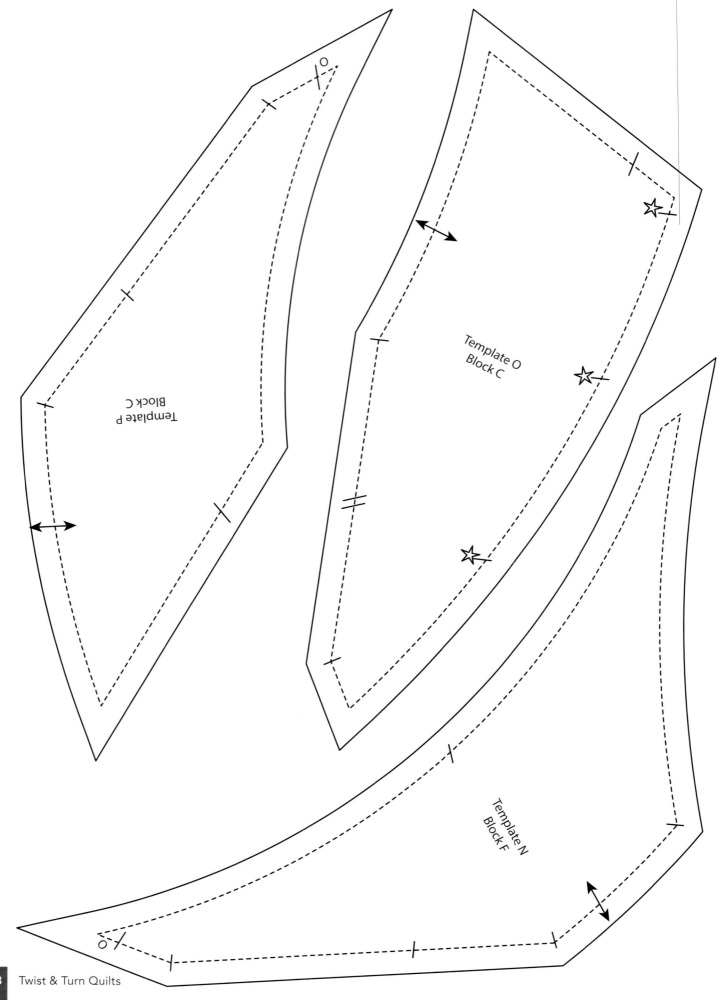

Template P
Block C

Template O
Block C

Template N
Block F

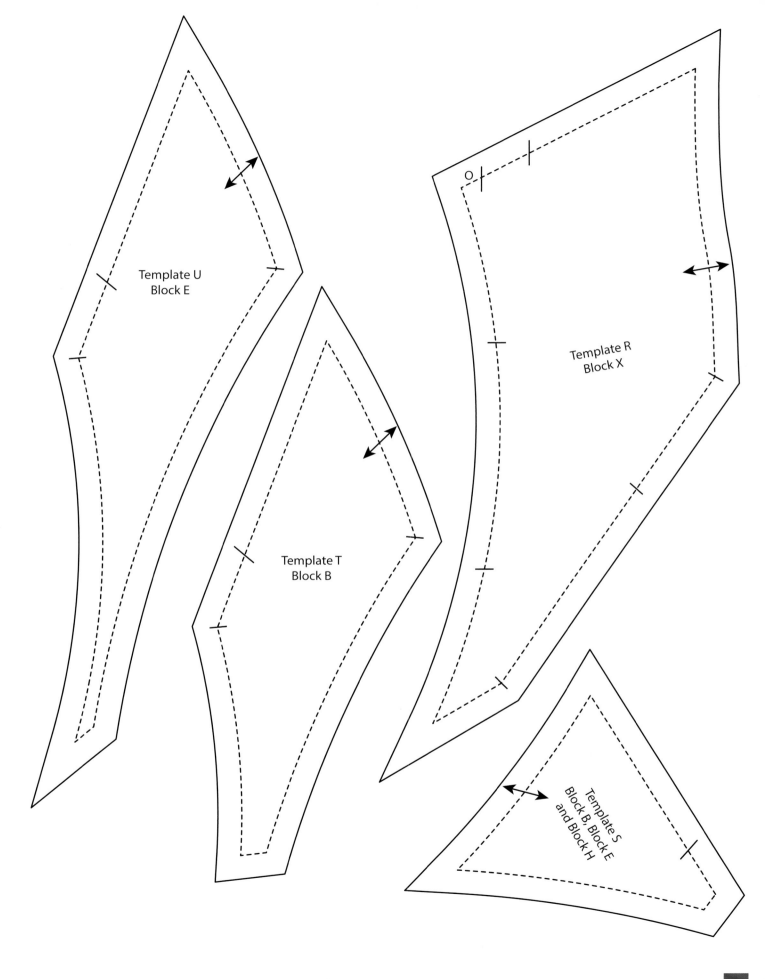

Template U
Block E

Template T
Block B

Template R
Block X

O

Template S
Block B, Block E
and Block H

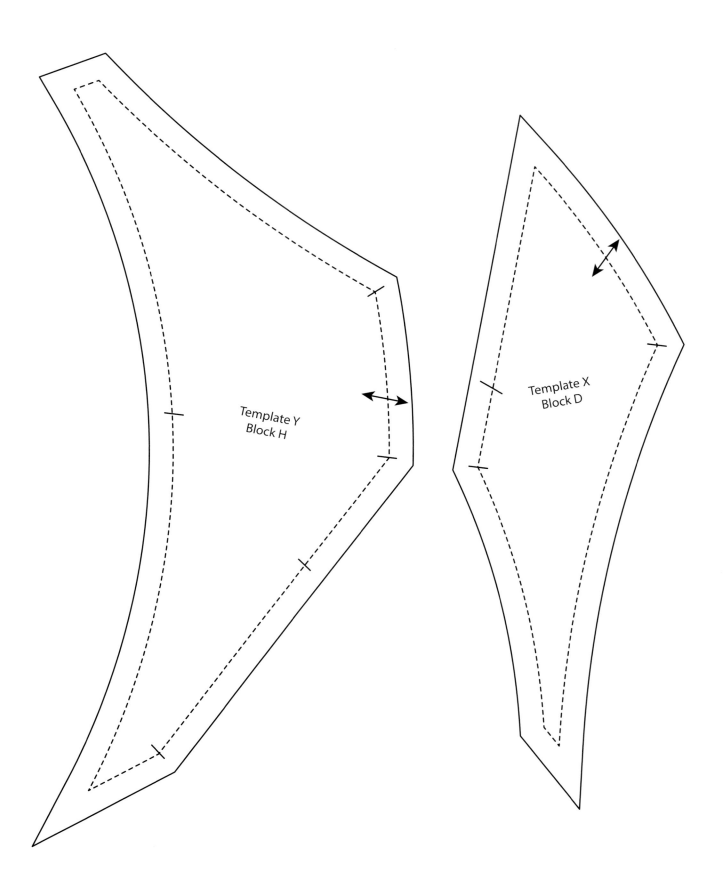

Template Y
Block H

Template X
Block D

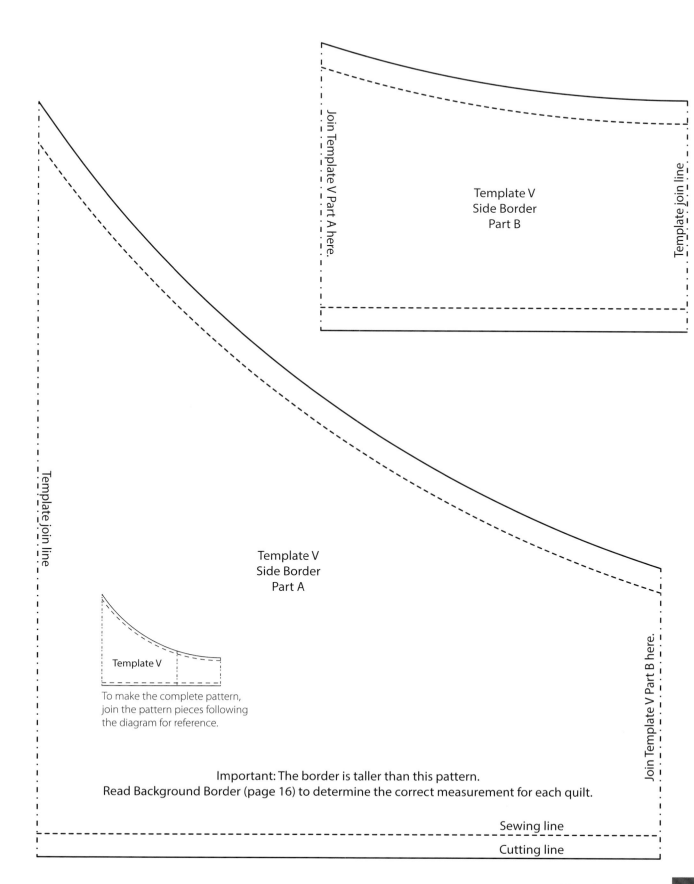

Template V
Side Border
Part B

Join Template V Part A here.

Template join line

Template V
Side Border
Part A

Template join line

Template V

To make the complete pattern,
join the pattern pieces following
the diagram for reference.

Join Template V Part B here.

Important: The border is taller than this pattern.
Read Background Border (page 16) to determine the correct measurement for each quilt.

Sewing line

Cutting line

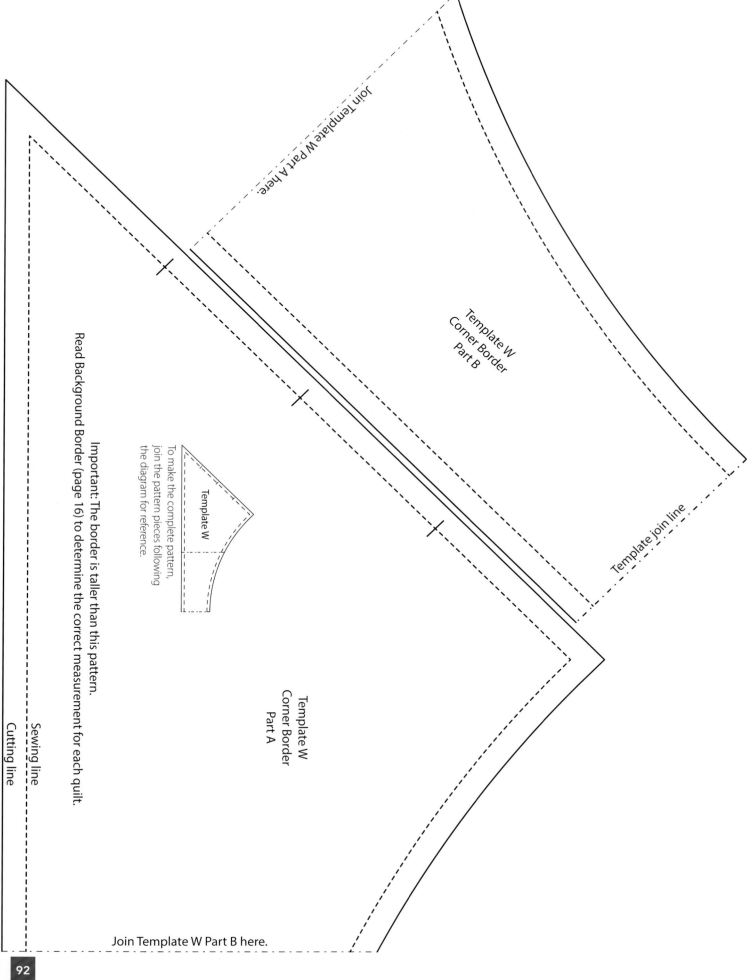

Join Template W Part A here.

Template W
Corner Border
Part B

Template join line

Template W

To make the complete pattern,
join the pattern pieces following
the diagram for reference.

Important: The border is taller than this pattern.
Read Background Border (page 16) to determine the correct measurement for each quilt.

Template W
Corner Border
Part A

Sewing line

Cutting line

Join Template W Part B here.

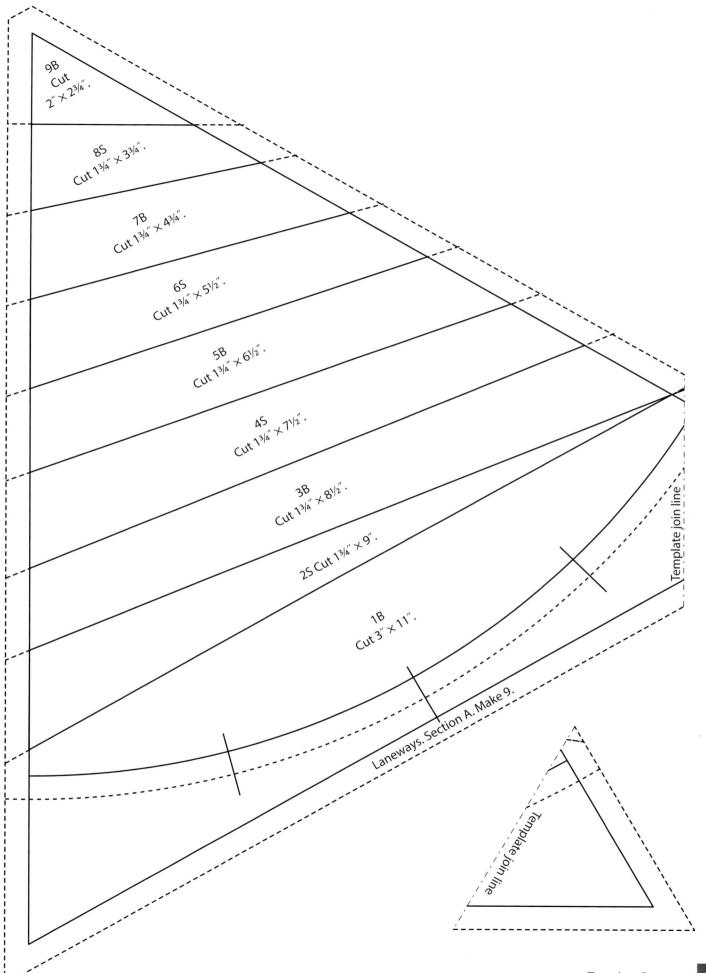

9B
Cut
2" × 2¾".

8S
Cut 1¾" × 3¾".

7B
Cut 1¾" × 4¾".

6S
Cut 1¾" × 5½".

5B
Cut 1¾" × 6½".

4S
Cut 1¾" × 7½".

3B
Cut 1¾" × 8½".

2S Cut 1¾" × 9".

1B
Cut 3" × 11".

Laneways. Section A. Make 9.

Template join line

Template join line

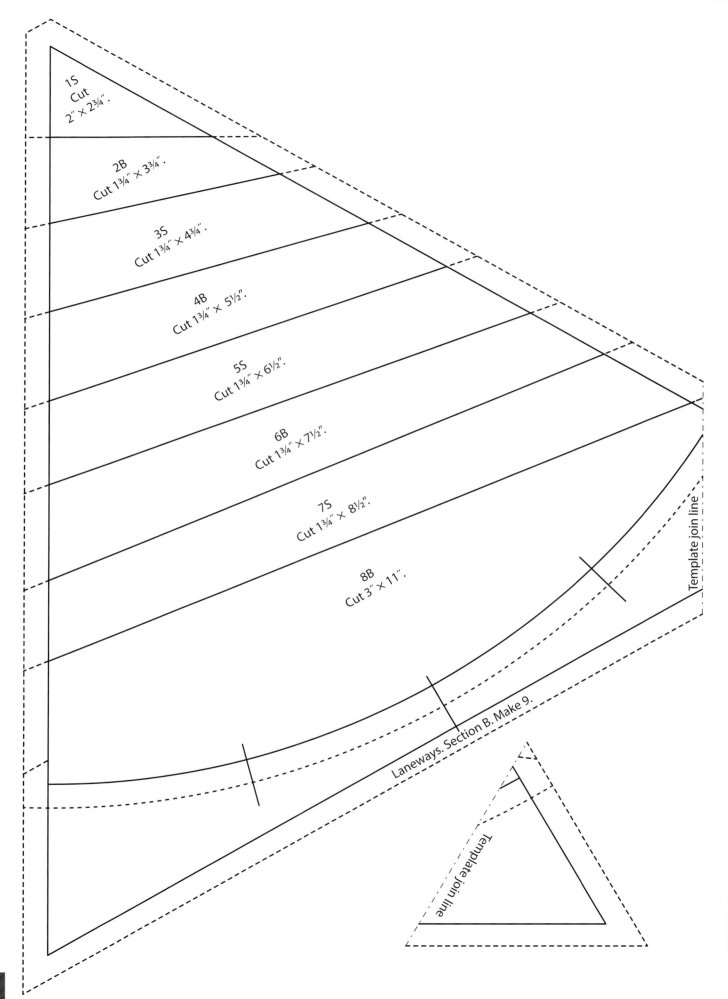

1S
Cut
2" × 2¾".

2B
Cut 1¾" × 3¾".

3S
Cut 1¾" × 4¾".

4B
Cut 1¾" × 5½".

5S
Cut 1¾" × 6½".

6B
Cut 1¾" × 7½".

7S
Cut 1¾" × 8½".

8B
Cut 3" × 11".

Template join line

Laneways, Section B. Make 9.

Template join line

About the Author

Cinzia White has been quilting for almost 35 years. This is her third book following on from her hexagon sampler, *The Storyteller's Sampler Quilt* (from C&T Publishing) and her New York Beauty sampler, *Dazzling New York Beauty Sampler Quilt* (from C&T Publishing). She has also published numerous patterns in Australian and American patchwork magazines and has taught throughout Australia.

Cinzia enjoys designing traditional quilts that are based on geometric designs and with perseverance and a desire to explore new directions, she has created many award-winning quilts. She prefers the variety that sampler quilts offer and so her quilts often include a large range of designs.

Cinzia loves working with color and often with no prearranged plan. She has a tendency to incorporate points and curves into her intricate patterns that alternate between 2 distinct styles: 1 scrappy and haphazard, the other involving intricate interlocking patterns.

Photo by Aimee Kirkham, Oxford Photography

Trails, the first quilt in this series was the result of a desire to explore something new with Flying Geese. The original quilt was designed for and made by hand piecing and quilting. When friends requested a smaller size that could be constructed using machine techniques Cinzia modified the templates and pattern slightly resulting in the many quilts presented here.

Cinzia lives in Gerringong, NSW Australia and may be found at the Facebook page **facebook.com/groups/cinziawhitedesigns**

The Trails *quilt has won many awards, including:*

Australia

2006 Victorian Quilt Show—1st place Professional Innovative Quilts

2006 Queensland Quilt Show—1st place Professional Traditional Quilts

2006 Quilt West—1st place Professional Traditional Quilts

2006 SA Festival of Quilts—2nd place Professional Bed Quilts

2005 NSW Quilt Show—1st place Professional Large Pieced Quilts

2005 NSW Quilt Show—2nd place Viewer's Choice

2005 Canberra Quilt Show—1st place Large Professional

Viewer's Choice at numerous local quilt shows

United States

Featured in *500 Traditional Quilts*, Lark Books, 2014

Exhibited by invitation at 2015 Quilt Festival, Houston, Texas; 2016 Quilt Festival, Chicago, Illinois; and numerous other U.S. quilt shows.

Toured the United States for 2 years.

CREATIVE SPARK
ONLINE LEARNING

Quilting courses to become an expert quilter...

From their studio to yours, Creative Spark instructors are teaching you how to create and become a master of your craft. So not only do you get a look inside their creative space, you also get to be a part of engaging courses that would typically be a one or multi-day workshop from the comfort of your home.

Creative Spark is not your one-size-fits-all online learning experience. We welcome you to be who you are, share, create, and belong.

Scan for a gift from us!

creativespark.ctpub.com